Forward Together

Lilly May

authorHOUSE®

AuthorHouse™ UK
1663 Liberty Drive
Bloomington, IN 47403 USA
www.authorhouse.co.uk
Phone: 0800.197.4150

Published by AuthorHouse 04/12/2019

ISBN: 978-1-5462-9862-5 (sc)
ISBN: 978-1-5462-9861-8 (e)

Print information available on the last page.

CONTENTS

Forward Together charts the lives of Lilly May and her husband, Michael, as a mixed married couple through some very interesting times and experiences. It's a record for their family or for anyone who wishes to read autobiographies about adventures ordinary men and women can experience in their own lives. This is a book of events and happenings that have occurred in Lilly May and Michael's everyday living; it share stories of holidays and their lives in military and civilian professions. *Forward Together* chronicles the ups and downs of following a soldier and the challenges of civilian life former military families have to adapt to. Lilly May expects readers can draw on their own happenings and events to relate and tell to others of their adventures and experiences.

Forward Together
Part 2 of Montego May,

a biography of a girl from Jamaica
This is Lilly May's second story.

Jamaica is an island where visitors flock in the thousands to soak up the hot tropical sunshine. They come to swim, scuba-dive, snorkel, or splash in the warm clear waters of the Caribbean Sea or to relax on soft white sands, trying to achieve that perfect tan. They come to drink the local rum and party into the small hours of the many hotels that run along the coast or to explore the lush green interior of the mountains and villages. This is the Jamaica that tourists know.

But it was a different story for the local population, whose lives were hard. Wages were low and exploitation, frequent. Those were the times in which I grew up. If you have come across my first book called *Montego May*, you know it told of the occasional good times that weaved in and out of my life. My friends persuaded me to write my story as a history for my own family. It showed how I and others were treated—looking at my experiences as a young girl and later as a young adult. This book is a continuation of my life story. I wrote so that, in later years, my children and their children will be able see how I managed, especially as a young mother, to bring up my family.

I have also changed the names of the people I have encountered to avoid embarrassment or discomfort for those who were not so kind.

CHAPTER 1

A Very Special Day

I was in Jamaica, and it was the day of my wedding. How could I ever forget that day? It was engraved on my heart, for my life was to change completely.

Gone were the anxious and pain-filled years of my childhood and teens. Gone were the tears and loneliness of a child without a mother. No more would I face hurt and insults from my relations and so-called friends. I was free. A new future stood before me. For on that day, I was to be married to a young English soldier on a tour of duty to Jamaica, which was still a part of the British Overseas Commonwealth that included many of the islands in the Caribbean.

I remember the day as if it were only yesterday—all the planning and preparations had come together, and there was nothing else to do but get into my wedding dress with the help of Mrs James, the lady who had made it. When we had finished, I looked into the long mirror, and there I was,

feeling like a princess. Mrs James had the largest beaming face of approval I had ever seen.

Then the realisation of what I was about to do set in. I was trembling and shaking with excitement and anxiety. But it was too late to change my mind now. There was the blare of a car horn outside the house. Mr Lewis, our chauffeur and friend, had kindly agreed to drive my uncle and me to the church, a well-known building in downtown Kingston. It was the Salvation Army Bramwell Booth Memorial Hall.

On arrival, we had to drive around the block several times before the maid of honour and bridesmaids arrived. They slipped quickly into the hall, and the scene was set. Uncle was at my side, ready to escort me up the steps into the cool, inviting interior of the hall.

Suddenly, there was a small commotion on the pavement outside of the hall, as a small, scruffy-looking man who must have seen Michael, my soon-to-be husband, and Darren, his best man, go into the hall. He was shouting at me, "Ga alang nah! Stick to ya own kine!"

But then a woman shouted back to him, "Shut yamout!" (Shut your mouth!) "Time for a change!"

All this I hardly noticed, as I was so focused on the ceremony that was to come. I was trembling as my uncle and I walked up the steps. My bouquet was shaking, my stomach was fluttering, and my knees felt weak.

On reaching the top step and going into the doorway, I stopped to try to compose myself. I looked towards the front of the hall, and there were Michael and Darren. They were looking very smart in their military white uniforms with gold-braid epaulettes across their shoulders and broad red stripes running down the length of their black well-pressed

trousers. All of this I saw in an instant, along with the many guests who had been invited to share this joyous day with us.

All heads were turned towards me, and as I stepped inside, one of my friends by the door said, "Oh, Miss May, you look beautiful!"

At that moment, my bouquet stopped shaking, the fluttering in my stomach disappeared, and gone was the weakness in my knees. The "Wedding March" started, and Uncle and I walked towards the front, down past the sea of people who wanted to catch my attention. Even my aunty-in-law, who had refused to make my wedding dress, touched me as I walked past.

And then I was there, side by side with Michael. Our eyes met, and we both smiled and then beamed with approval of each other's wedding outfits.

In front of us was Captain Neeson, a tall Canadian who conducted the marriage ceremony. (Ranks were used by the Salvation Army, instead of vicar or pastor.) There was a bit of giggling on our part when "for better or for worse, for richer or poorer" was read out. That made everyone smile and relax to take in the serious and meaningful occasion.

With the rings exchanged and the vows completed, we stepped forward as man and wife—as Mr and Mrs Green. I was walking on clouds of happiness.

I knew what the staff at the school, the Salvation Army School for the Blind and Visually Handicapped, were saying: "It will never work. "He only wants her to cook, wash, iron, and clean when he gets back to England." "She only wants to marry him to get a one-way ticket to England." Many other unkind and jealous remarks had come to my hearing.

All that was now behind me. I no longer had to put up

with the jibes and cruel remarks that had been directed at me during my time at the school. My future was now in the hands of another, a man I wanted to spend the rest of my life with.

Our reception was held at the Salvation Army School for the Blind and Visually Handicapped, which had the quaint address of 19½ Slipe Pen Road, Kingston. How we got there I don't know, as our minds were in a blur. Our eighty-six guests were there waiting for us, and the dining room was beautifully transformed to rows of tables with dazzling white tablecloths and an array of gleaming cutlery and matching tableware. This was due to the two most wonderful people I had come to know and to love. I looked on them as "Mum and Dad." They were Captain and Mrs Wicks, who were the managers of the school. They had arranged, organised, and paid for our wedding from start to finish. Numerous times I had a run-in with the staff (who hated me) and was ready to leave, Mrs Wicks, somehow in her soft voice of wisdom and reason, persuaded me to stay and see through the bad and rough times. Many years later, they both died within a short time of one another. Even now, I still miss them.

There was one incident during the reception that I still remember to this day. My uncle brought a wedding cake with friends and neighbours in a car from Montego Bay. It was the contribution of him and all the people who knew me to our wedding. We already had one wedding cake lovingly prepared by Captain and Mrs Wicks, which was placed at the top table. We found out later when it was the coolest part of the day, they would try to ice the cake before it got

too hot and the icing became runny, and would come down at 4.30 in the morning.

When Uncle's cake was put out, this rich powerful aroma of rum permeated every corner of the dining area. Now the Salvation Army does not allow spirits of any kind, and when the cakes were cut, the first one to disappear was—yes, you've guessed it—the cake with the rum. Who cut it up and distributed it, we never knew, but it had vanished before we could say the word *rum*.

Looking back, I (as I'm sure most brides do) have locked in my memories of the precious moments of happiness and love on my special day, believing mine was the best wedding ever.

The wedding was over, the reception was done, the presents were collected, and we made our way down to 23 Sackville Road, our first home. It was a little bungalow on hire behind a big house that was owned by Cubans and at the bottom of Up Park Camp, where Michael had been living in barracks.

The Move to
Marrion Avenue

Weeks earlier, he and his friends had worked hard on the place. They gave it new paint, new electrics, and other alterations, changing a rather dark and grubby building to a bright, clean, and fully restored residence. I was so proud of my own little place. It was the first I could ever call our own. Although rented, it was our own little palace.

We spent many happy months there, but I used to get lonely when Michael pedalled off to the barracks, leaving me with a day to fill. How I worked, scrubbing and polishing the floors until they shone with mirror-like reflections. I cleaned windows until the glass was so clear it seemed as if there were no windowpanes to look through. I washed the whites and let them bleach in the sun so even a saint would have been pleased to wear them. Or you could say I washed them as white as snow. But that was just an expression to me, as I didn't know what snow was.

One hot afternoon, while I was relaxing on top of the

bed and feeling the waft of cooling air from the overhead fan, suddenly there was a commotion outside. I heard shouting and running. Getting up to see what was happening; I went to the door and was told to stay inside. There was a prisoner on the loose, who'd run under the bottom of the big house, which was raised off the ground to keep it cool. The police had been called, and the prisoner was soon captured, put in chains, and taken away. If I had kept my front door unlocked, he may have run in and held me as a hostage.

That event unsettled me. Suddenly, my little castle did not seem so secure anymore. I did not sleep as well; the days when Michael went off to work seemed longer. The slightest noise or bump from outside in the yard put me on edge. And I wanted to get away to a safer and more populated area.

One day, as I was talking to a woman who I knew slightly, she mentioned there was a place for rent not too far from where we were living. She knew I was no longer happy at our little bungalow behind the big house. I decided to go and take a look for myself. The location was Marrion Avenue, but she was uncertain which house it was. I found the avenue and asked several people in the area what place was on offer to rent. I was directed to a duplex house, which was a dwelling that had apartments with separate entrances for two families. The landlady showed me around bright clean airy rooms, which had tiled floors throughout. The place gave off a cool feeling and a pleasant atmosphere. The house was in a yard (Jamaican expression for a shared area) with lots of people around and wasn't too far from the shops.

I could hardly wait until Michael got home. I excitedly told him about the new home I had found. He wasn't so sure but reluctantly agreed to go and see the place for himself.

He and his friends from the army had put a lot of work into where we lived, but he knew I was no longer content at Sackville Road. Michael, on seeing the house himself, seemed pleasantly surprised. We agreed, if the price was right, we would move in.

A few weeks later the move was made. I felt comfortable and secure in my new home. The neighbours were friendly, and there was lots of activity around the yard. One particular incident comes to mind when Michael and I were having a lively "pillow fight," with lots of screams, laughing, and shouting. We eventually called it a draw, tidied, and cleared up the many feathers that were lying around and went to bed. The next morning when he had gone to work, our neighbour called round looking very concerned and worried. She'd heard shouting and screaming coming through the walls the night before, and was I all right? Laughingly, I told her about the pillow fight, and I could see the relief showing in her face.

Another time, it was in the cool of the evening, and we were sitting in the veranda playing drafts. The neighbours got to find out that this was a game of drafts with a difference. This was a battle to see who would take the dustbin out to the front gate in the morning. I lost the game.

The next day, under orders from the "Drafts King," I had to struggle along the path with a big heavy galvanised dustbin full of rubbish. As I was doing this, many of the neighbours came to their doors and cheered me on.

That's how it was during those happy days at Marrion Avenue.

Now that year, growing demands for Jamaican independence were in the air, and political meetings were gathering force, sometimes with rowdy or violent behaviour.

CHAPTER 3

The Last English Regiment in Jamaica

Britain was withdrawing its troops from several parts of the Caribbean and Michael's regiment was given orders to leave the island before 1963, when the island was to be given its own self-government. The final farewell parade was held on the large polo field just below the barracks. All the officers and soldiers were lined up in three ranks stretching the length of the long field. The regiment's commanding officer stood on a raised dais, prepared to take the farewell salute. The band was at the top end ready to march them off.

Suddenly all three lines started to wobble and waver. Some soldiers almost fell over and the RSM (regimental sergeant major) was screaming, "Stand still. Stand still." But of course you can't stop an earth tremor as it ripples up through a field. It was all over in about five seconds, and order and dignity was restored again. The regimental band struck up, and the troops marched off for the last time.

After that, we were busy packing what little we had and

making arrangements for the furniture that had been hired to be collected. Now the worries set in. Where were we going to live? Michael did not qualify for a married quarter, as we'd only been married for a short time and, according to the army system, we had not built up enough points to be eligible.

The hot sunny days passed by. Rumours and counter-rumours came and went as to when we were actually leaving. Then at last a date was given. The main body of the regiment was flying back to England in May 1962.

The day finally arrived, and buses took us to Palisadoes Airport. Today's tourists know it as Norman Manley International Airport. Michael and I boarded the Britannia Aircraft (whispering giants as they were known), and we waited and waited for take-off. We sat for hours in the hot stifling body of the plane. Babies were crying, mothers were getting distressed, and everyone was sweating because the air conditioning was not working.

After what was an age, we had to get off the plane. We found out the flight engineer had tripped and had broken his ankle. We emerged hot and dripping with sweat and were transported back to camp to be allocated different hotels in the Montego Bay area. The officers and senior ranks were given the Turtle Bank Hotel, one of the more luxurious hotels around the Bay. We and others were placed in the Thatham Hotel and additional hotels for an overnight stay.

The next day, on returning to the plane, we heard that the exclusive Turtle Bank was not quite the place it was made out to be. Some showers were not working properly. Various suites seemed cramped, and there were beds that seemed uncomfortable. At breakfast, there were long queues

and not much of a breakfast selection. Meanwhile, we lesser mortals had comfortable rooms, excellent service, and a choice of lots of different breakfast selections. (I hasten to add this was then in 1962. If the Turtle Bank Hotel is still in operation, it is probably up there with the exclusive five-star standards.)

A replacement engineer was found, and we settled down for the long haul to the United Kingdom. As we roared down the runway, I wondered if I would ever see my beautiful country again. We climbed up into the warm blue sky, and as the plane circled and dipped to one side, I could see the lush green tropical countryside below me slip away. I felt a lump in my throat. I was leaving the country of my birth for a new and distant land.

The flight to England was uneventful. The plane droned through the night. Then in the morning, the announcement to fasten our seat belts was called, and we were on the final touchdown to London Heathrow. We descended through thick heavy grey clouds and finally landed at the airport in the cold damp climate of a late English spring

CHAPTER 4

Meeting the Family

I still remember it to this day. As we got to the door to leave the aircraft, it was as if someone had thrown a bucket of icy water over me. I couldn't believe and didn't realise it could be so cold. I was wearing a thin short-sleeved jacket and skirt, which looked very nice in Jamaica but was totally inadequate for the English climate. I could hear the wives behind me saying, "Oh! It's freezing; let's get back to sunny Jamaica," as they too reluctantly left the plane.

The day itself was dull, bleak, and overcast, with a stiff breeze that made the temperature even cooler. After clearing customs, we caught a train to Basingstoke in Hampshire; Michael's family lived a few miles outside the town at what was then a small country village called East Oakley. I was shivering and wondered if I would ever be warm again. Mike took off his jacket and put it round me. It helped but then I was worried that he would be cold.

I was getting strange looks from people on the train. I didn't realise at the time it was because I was black and not

many of us were seen in trains and buses at that time. This was before many Jamaicans and others had come to that part of the county in large numbers.

When we arrived at Basingstoke, the first thing Michael did was to find a boutique that sold coats. I tried on several, finally settling on a warm pink fluffy one that fitted me perfectly. It was the first coat that I had ever owned, for in Jamaica they were never used. Oh! I had a wonderful feeling of warmth which surrounded me as I snuggled into its fleecy interior. He also bought some warm woollen gloves, which I had never ever used before. I felt I could go out now and meet the world.

We got a taxi to where Michael's father lived. There at the door was his dad. The family must have been looking through the window to see us arrive. He looked very smart in his suit and highly polished shoes. I thought he was going out, but Mike assured me he always dressed like that.

Introductions were made to him and the rest of the family, who were waiting to see me. There was his aunty, his cousin Sheila, and his formidable grandmother—a lady with fixed ideas that dated back to her Victorian middle-class upbringing. She ruled over the family with an iron fist.

After the exchange of greetings, we had a proper English tea made up of little sandwiches cut into corners and tea served from a very dainty teapot. I would have loved to have kept my pink coat on, as it was cool in the house. But because of my nervousness and little understanding of English etiquette, I felt I had better not say anything. So I shivered in silence.

I did get the general impression they were assessing me and seeing if I was good enough to be accepted into the

family. With Michael's father it went well. I could tell he liked me. But I was never really sure about the aunt, the cousin, and Grandma. It was all very polite and small talk.

Then shortly afterwards, Michael's sister and her husband (Sheila and Nathan) turned up to take us back to their place, where we were to stay for a while. Mike had not found a house for us yet and was still trying. So the plan was to stay with his sisters, Sheila, Jeanne, and Barbara until we had an army quarters or found a home of our own.

When we got to Sheila and Nathan's place, she told us that she'd told her little daughter, Greta, who was three at the time, that I was a different colour from all the other people she knew. When I got to meet her, she stared and stared in amazement. I was so completely unlike her friends and family. But we fast became friends, and she accepted me for who I was.

I quickly settled into my new surroundings at Highlands Road in Worthington (near Basingstoke). Sheila and Nathan made me feel as comfortable as possible. Michael had gone back to the camp at Crookham, and I only saw him at the weekends. It is strange how little things stick in your mind.

CHAPTER 5

From Pillar to Post

Even after all these years, I can still recall my first Sunday with Nathan and Sheila. When dinner arrived, it was lamb, potatoes, greens, and gravy. It looked very small, as I was used to the huge dinners of salt fish and ackee, sweet potatoes, yam, rice, plantain, peppers, and callaloo (the spinach-like leaves of a tropical American plant, used in Caribbean cooking), which taste spinach like. In Jamaica, we hardly ever bothered with dessert, for after eating a full and filling dinner, there was no room for anything else.

Sheila's dessert was rhubarb and custard. I had never heard of it. I had never seen it or tasted it. So it was a strange new experience, among the many I encountered during my early years in England. Sheila, on seeing my face, asked me if I liked it. I respectfully said, "Yes." But she wasn't fooled and said, "Was it sweet enough?" I just smiled, but I found it rather sharp and sour. She sprinkled on some more sugar, which made it a little sweeter and a little better. Then she

took me down the garden to show me what rhubarb looked like.

The days passed slowly, and how I missed Michael. I was always talking about my little family of blind girls back home where I worked, and he found an ad in the papers seeking a live-in nanny at a home for maladjusted children. He applied for me, and soon I had a letter asking me to attend for an interview. Sheila's husband drove us to this rather gloomy and rambling house way out in the countryside. Several days later, I had a letter from the place asking me when I could start. I was a little apprehensive but excited that I would be working with children again.

Not long into the work, I found out it was a terrible mistake. The children were treated badly, not physically but mentally, with the wrongdoers being publically humiliated in front of everyone. One little boy had wet his bed and was brought up in front of the whole school. He was told to stay in the hall all morning and then go and wash his sheets. It was not a happy place, with running laughing children—not like I was used to at the Salvation Army School in Jamaica. There was always hilarity, jokes, and freedom of expression. How I loved those little girls, and it was such a wrench when I left for England. This home was almost a throwback to Dickensian times, where children walked in fear and the staffs were harsh or severe.

I recall two young women—Swedish I think?—who worked at the home. They were lovely. They too did not like the way the children were treated. I don't know what happened to them because I was so unhappy that I asked Nathan to come and pick me up and take me back to their house. I had seen enough of the treatment that was given

out to those poor little children, and I didn't even wait for my wages.

Michael was away again, this time at Aldershot on a physical training course to become an assistant physical training instructor, so I saw even less of him than before. I was finding it hard to be a "soldier's wife".

We had an invite to go and visit his youngest sister, Barbara, and her husband, Derek, who lived in Chelmsford. We caught a train down to Essex, and there on the platform they were waiting to meet us. Excited introductions were made. Barbara even introduced us to one another, saying, "Michael, this is Lilly May, and Lilly May, this is Michael," she was so flustered.

After hugs and kisses, I said to her "Oh, Barbara, you are so lovely, big, and meaty," giving her a Jamaican compliment.

There was a stunned silence and shocked look on her face, and then I realised in England this was not a compliment; on the contrary, it was an insult. I quickly apologised, and she broke out laughing, realising that it wasn't meant in malice. That was another English custom I quickly learnt.

We were only at Barbara and Derek's house for a short while, but it was nice getting to know all of the family. Arrangements were made for me to go to stay with his middle sister, Jeanne, and husband, Johnny.

The weather was turning colder, as autumn started to make a show of all the colours of leaves—a sight never seen in Jamaica, as the trees are always a lush tropical green. I was spellbound by the golds, greens, yellows, and browns the trees displayed with their showy colours. Another thing

I found fascinating was the long evening hours of daylight in the summer, when the sun seemed to hang in the sky forever. Back home, it started to get dark round about 6 p.m., and by 7 p.m., it was night, with the stars glowing. The moon, if it was out, was a golden yellow sphere, and the cicadas would be chirping away in the bushes and a warm breeze wafting gently through the air.

October gave way to November, and I saw Mike at weekends only, to disappear on Sunday evenings. Jeanne and Johnny tried very hard to make me feel at home but I really did miss my husband.

From Pillar to Post Again

The weather was turning cold as December crept in, and whenever I went out, it was always in my lovely warm pink coat. One day, I was standing at the window when I saw what I thought was ash coming from a chimney fire. I said to Johnny, "Oh look. Somebody's chimney is on fire."

He took a look and said, "That isn't ash, May. It's snow. Come with me." He added, "Get your coat, and we'll go and see."

We went down the stairs to the front garden, and there before me was my first sight of snow. There in the cold still air was this thin layer of white powdery substance, floating down slowly and silently settling everywhere. I scooped up a handful and tasted it. No! It wasn't like ice cream. It wasn't like ice cubes. It was sort of frozen rainwater, which just melted in your mouth. I was so excited. I had read about it in books. I had seen it on Christmas cards with pictures of snow everywhere. We had watched men in films battling against howling winds and blinding snow. But this was

the real thing I was actually experiencing my first sight, sensation, and taste of snow.

Michael was not having much luck finding us a place for ourselves, and I was beginning to feel uncomfortable and restless. Then realised I was pregnant. What was I going to do? Michael had a friend called Ryan going right back to when they were schoolboys together. The two had kept in touch for many years. He asked Ryan if we could stay at Ryan and his wife's house until he had found somewhere for us. This was agreed, and a short time later I was taken to their place just outside of Fleet in Hampshire and settled in.

Ryan's wife did not accept me at all and always seemed cold and distant. They had a young baby called Eric and very often I was left to do the babysitting while they went out. One day, while carrying Eric downstairs, I tripped and fell and skidded all the way to the bottom on my back, holding onto the baby on my stomach to protect him. He was screaming with fright, and I was badly shaken.

When I told Ryan's wife what had happened when she returned from playing tennis, she quickly took him from me, cuddled him, and kept him on her lap—not a word to ask how I was.

The next morning, I thought I had better get to the doctor's to have myself checked out, as I was about three months pregnant by then. The walk to the doctor's was a very long one, and Ryan's wife did not offer me a lift in her car. I felt very tired when I got there.

After a long wait, a doctor called me and checked me over. He was very sympathetic and seemed satisfied that my baby was intact and safe. Oh how my back hurt, especially on the long walk back to the house.

Another time, I was explaining to Ryan how we cooked and seasoned our meat in my country. He asked me to cook him some beef Jamaican style. I knew he spent a lot of time at his mother's, and she served him up good man-sized dinners, as his wife's cooking was very plain and very little. While I was there, I existed mainly on toast, cheese, and tomatoes. This was nearly every day, despite the fact I was pregnant. I was not getting enough proper wholesome food for two. It was a Saturday when Ryan came home. He brought a large piece of prime beef, saying he would really be looking forward to it for Sunday lunch. I was so excited I could hardly sleep that night, thinking how I was going to marinate and prepare the beef to cook in the morning. Needless to say, his wife got up very early the next day and put the beef straight in to the oven as it was. When challenged by Ryan, her reply was that she "forgot". He was very angry with her. It was not a happy time there.

There came an invitation to stay with friends down on the South Coast for a week or two, which I quickly accepted. They were friends we'd both known when we were in Jamaica. Their children, Joy and Mary, were our bridesmaids. Just before we left to see our friends, Mike had a run-in with Ryan, as he wanted to charge us full rent for the one small room we had, even though I would not be there. We'd thought that, given their friendship, he would charge us half or none for the two weeks I would be away. But no! He was adamant he wanted a full payment of rent. Michael was very angry, as he and Ryan had been such close friends in earlier days.

Alex, our friend, had a weekend off and came all the way from down south to collect me, as my husband was

still away. We took the lengthy drive down, mainly using the old A308 road. The drive seemed to go on forever. We made many stops, as my baby was pressing on my bladder, and my "bump" was definitely growing. Staying with Alex and Carla was wonderful and so relaxing. And I wasn't stuck with babysitting duties or just sitting in that one room wishing that my husband could be with me. Plus, eating proper meals was a tonic I really needed.

The Caravan Incident

All too soon, that happy time came to an end, and I was back to the tensions and strains at Ryan's house. Because of the bad feelings that had occurred, I did find some relief thanks to Ryan's mother' She was a kind and maternal lady, and I used to spend time with her occasionally. So it was still a "pillar-to-post" situation.

Finally, Mike managed to get a caravan for us to stay in. I remember it oh so well. It was in a scruffy-looking field in the middle of nowhere, with rather tired and dilapidated caravans dotted around and only a few basic facilities. There was water and electricity. No flush toilet, no fridge, and a coke fire that gave off more fumes than heat. It was called Western Rough Caravan Estate—not a good place to be. But it was the perfect name for the site. I am sure it must have since been closed down by the health and safety authorities or brought up to a decent standard.

By this time, I was getting morning sickness, which lasted well into the afternoons, and could hardly keep

anything down. When Mike came back at nights, he would coax me to have something, only to bring it back up half an hour later. Our caravan always had the smell of lavender mist aerosol, to try and mask the odour of me being constantly sick. Even now after all those years ago, whenever I smell lavender it brings back memories of those not-so-happy days in the caravan.

One cold December morning, there was knocking at the door. A man and woman were standing there, demanding to know what we were doing in their caravan? They had come down from London and wanted to tow it away. It appeared the site manager had illegally rented us someone else's caravan. There was a big argument with the manager, and the people wanted to call the police, and I was stuck in the middle of it. Michael, of course, was nowhere around, and it looked like I was going to be homeless again.

A very kind man said he had a spare caravan, and we could stay there for a while until we had sorted out our accommodation. He helped me move our belongings to the new place, and Mike had a real shock when he got back from work. There were no mobile phones in those days, so communication was very slow. He was very angry at the distress I had been put through and, the next day, demanded to see his family officer and explain the situation.

It appeared to have worked, for the orderly room (administration block) was told to come up with an answer for Private Green by the end of the week. Well, it was a sort of answer. There was an army hostel up in Blackpool, apparently a very good one, and there was a room available for me to stay. I could move in at any time. The main stumbling point was that Michael was on his physical

training course in Aldershot in Hampshire, and I was to be sent up to Blackpool in Lancashire.

My interview about marrying a soldier in Jamaica with the adjutant, who had piercing blue eyes, came flooding back to me. "A soldier's wife can find it very hard to fit in with the comings and goings of military life," he'd told me.

A short time after the caravan incident, the orderly room contacted the army hostel, telling the managers to expect me the following weekend. All our worldly possessions were packed into our rather elderly Morris Minor, and we set off for Blackpool some 140 miles (225 kilometres) away. The journey was long, with frequent "bladder" stops for my "bump."

On passing through the small market town of Wellington in Shropshire, I thought I saw a man I knew from my Jamaica days. Mike stopped the car, and I called him over. I was right. I recognised him as Mr Ray Simmons. We exchanged a few pleasantries and then set off on our way again.

I later learnt that Mr Simmons thought we were off on a "dirty weekend" when he wrote to his sister in Jamaica, as he saw all my clothes piled on the back seat of our car. He was quickly put right by return of post when his sister explained that we had been married in Jamaica.

CHAPTER 8

Snow and More Snow

Our journey was long and tedious, and we eventually arrived at the hostel on Palatine Road just as the light was fading and a grey mist was closing in. Mr and Mrs Withington, the owners of the hostel, were expecting me and made me feel so welcome with typical Lancashire hospitality and warmth. They were under the impression that I had just arrived from Jamaica and wanted me to be warm and feel welcomed.

I quickly settled in to the place and found there two other families staying there. One was German, with five children. Her husband was in Aldershot. The other lady, whose husband was in Aden, had three children. He was stationed in the Middle East, which later became South Yemen People's Republic.

My room was small but adequate. Mr and Mrs Withington, who went by "Aunty and Uncle Whit", even had a wall heater fitted so I wouldn't feel the cold so much. Mind you, I had to feed two shillings (ten pence) into the

meter when I wanted it on, which did not seem to last very long. We had a communal dining room, and the food was hot and plenty. Aunty and Uncle Whit were a warm and loving couple, who did their best to make us feel at home.

Although the other wives were pleasant and easy to get on with, I still felt lonely, as Mike was so far away. I so looked forward to his visits, which were infrequent, as his army physical training course in Aldershot kept him busy.

The weeks slipped by, and the weather was getting colder. Christmas came and went. Christmas Day was a low-key affair, as Aunty and Uncle Whit were Jehovah's Witnesses and did not recognise the birth of Jesus Christ. Jehovah's Witnesses do not celebrate Christmas, owing to the fact that Christmas Day was originally a pagan Roman festival of Saturnalia, which was later to become a Christian celebration with the birth of Jesus.

Michael could not get up to see me because our car was giving trouble and the weather was very bad, even worse down in Southern England than in Blackpool. In late December, a blizzard swept across the country and, by the end of the year, covered most of the United Kingdom, as many will remember. That winter was the most severe on record, with temperatures falling to –24 degrees Celsius in early January. It held the record for the coldest in the United Kingdom since 1947. This cold spell lasted for about three months, blocking roads and railways, stranding villages, and bringing down power lines. The snow was reported to be up to twenty feet (nearly 7 metres) deep in parts of Southern England and Wales.

What on earth had I come in to with this horrible English weather? It was a difficult time for everyone. And as

for me, I was getting bigger and bigger. It was now February, the papers and news reports were full of disaster stories about the terrible conditions the country was suffering. I was becoming nervous over the impending birth of my baby.

In the middle of the month, I was admitted to the maternity wing of Glenroyd Hospital (now closed down), so the nurses could monitor me. I remember during a prenatal check, a nurse, when checking my stomach, pulled her hand away quickly. "Oh Lord," she said. "I can almost shake hands with the baby." She ran off to get a doctor.

The doctor came, felt my stomach, and laughed saying, "It's a good thing I worked in a gynaecology department in Jamaica. The stomach lining in a West Indian is thinner than in Europeans. That's why you could feel the foetus, but everything is fine."

The staffs at Glenroyd were marvellous. They all did their best to make me feel comfortable. They even put me in a side ward usually reserved for private patients.

CHAPTER 9

A Blackpool Baby

In February 1963, I went in to labour. It was a long, drawn-out, painful affair. The following day around noon, our precious daughter was born. She was a tiny perfectly formed beautiful baby, with masses of black hair. More than anything, I wanted Michael to be at my side full of pride as the baby's father. We had decided that, if it was a girl, her name was to be Aline. If we'd had a boy, his name would have been Anthony. So this tiny precious bundle named Aline came into a world that was held in the iron grasp of an Arctic winter that was the coldest in England since 1947.

The headlines for that year, 1963, were saying There was an embargo in place by the US government on Cuba. John Glen became the first American to orbit the earth in three hours. Heavy storms in Germany along the North Sea coast caused massive flooding, killing 300 people and leaving thousands homeless. A military coup took place in Burma,(now Myanmar) ousting the then prime minister and replacing the government, with a military junta taking

over the country. Snow brought Britain to a standstill and caused many disruptions and hardships. So it was a world full of trials and unrest to which Aline made her entry.

Mike at last managed to get up and see me after a gruelling seven-hour train journey, with snow piled high both sides of the track and sitting in a cold, draughty unheated carriage. Oh! I was overjoyed to see him and so wanted to show off our precious daughter. On seeing her, he really looked the proud father, with a grin wider than Morecambe Bay. He managed to get three days leave. And how quickly the time passed. The good news was that he had passed his physical training course and was posted to Shropshire as an instructor at the Junior Infantry Regiment at Park Hall Camp.

CHAPTER 10

Plas Hixon

The time had come for me to leave the warmth, comfort, and friendship of Mr and Mrs Withington and the army hostel in Blackpool and follow my husband to our new place outside Oswestry. He had found us an army hiring so we could at least be together. It was a big gloomy farmhouse called Plas Hixon (Welsh for "the large house of Mr Hixon"). It was about five miles (eight kilometres) from the camp, situated in the middle of nowhere, down a long drive, hidden by trees and surrounding fields and woods.

On arrival at the address, we found a warm welcoming fire in the hearth prepared by the young couple who lived on the other side of the house. The farmhouse was always cold and draughty. At nights, we kept Aline in the bottom drawer of a large chest of drawers so she was covered all round and protected from the icy blasts of air that rushed through the gaps in the floorboards. It was there I learnt to make up a fire in the hearth.

For a while, I was happy but again lonely, as Mike would

leave early in the morning and not return until after 6 p.m. from work. Some nights, he would not be home at all, as he was on duty in the camp. I hardly ever saw the other young couple occupying the other half of the building, as they both worked. The husband worked for the Milk Marketing Board and would leave round about 6 a.m. And the lady would leave the house promptly at eight. On most days, I would accompany her down the long drive to the bus stop.

I used to clean and tidy the house, polish the floor, and struggle to get the fire lit. I used to take walks down lonely snow-filled county lanes with my baby in her pram to pass away the time and to get her off to sleep.

She was always a crying baby, and some nights I was exhausted for lack of sleep. Night after night I would be kept awake by her non-stop crying. Oh I was so tired. One night, the young couple was going out for a meal. I saw them from the bedroom and waved. Hours later when they returned, she was still crying. I think I was on the point of a breakdown; such was the condition I was in.

I took her to the doctors to see if she was ill. But no, she was a normal healthy baby. But I do remember the nurse saying, "As soon as she gets her own room, she will stop crying."

I didn't really believe her.

The days slowly passed, and gradually winter released its grip on the freezing conditions that covered the country. By March the big thaw set in, leaving Britain in a flooded, battered, and snow-damaged condition.

CHAPTER 11

Moving into an Army Quarter

Oh joy of joys! We were eventually allocated an army quarter. It was much farther out than Plas Hixon, but it was to be our home for the foreseeable future. Our house was in the village of Highcliffe, which was a satellite housing estate for the main married quarters at Up Park Camp (now long disappeared). We had neighbours on either side of the street. Kingsway made up the other part of the little estate. We had a small NAAFI (Navy, Army, and Air Force Institutes) that was a shop for military personnel. There was a doctor's surgery nearby and a regular bus service in to Oswestry to get our weekly groceries. It was a pleasant place to be—so much better than the cold dark lonely farmhouse we had formerly lived in, where a butcher called once a week and a long walk to the main road was required to catch a bus. The only living things I had seen at that place were the butcher and the cows as they came past the window for milking in

a big barn, along with the occasional owl, sometimes a deer in the fields, and the young couple from time to time.

The army term for moving in to an army quarter was called a "march in". And although we have done many march ins since, we always will remember our first. All was spic and span. Everything was laid out for inspection in military fashion. The floors were highly polished, the bedding was laid out, and the cutlery and utensils were polished and ready to be checked.

Furniture was set out in each room. The BIA (barrack inventory accountant) checked off each item before passing on to the next. It took about an hour and a half to go through the quarter. But when the inspection was finished, the place was ours.

The first thing I did was to take Aline up to the smallest room and put her in the cot, complete with bedding that had been provided by the army. In those days, the army provided you with everything you needed—furniture for every room, bedding, pots and pans, cutlery, crockery, carpets, curtains, and garden tools. All you had to do was occupy the house, and you were ready to live in it. We settled her down and gently closed the door, leaving it just ajar to catch any sound or crying.

Mike and I busied ourselves, arranging the quarter how we wanted it to be. Finally, very tired, we went to bed. I peeped in at Aline, who looked as if she had never moved from the position I had first placed her in.

The next morning, I awoke with a start. I had actually had a full night's sleep. I went to check on her. But no! She was still sleeping.

We had breakfast. By this time I was getting worried,

for there was no crying or noise from our baby. I went to see if she was all right, fearing something dreadful had happened. Still no movements, so I started tickling her feet. She finally stirred and stretched. Oh what a relief.

At last she woke. So the nurse in Oswestry had been right after all. She would sleep soundly in her own bed.

CHAPTER 12

On the Move Once Again

We spent a pleasant spring and summer at Nesscliffe. At weekends, we would tour the Welsh countryside in our ancient Morris Minor car, visiting Lake Vyrnwy or Bala Lake. We'd drive to Llangollen or picnic by the Canal at Chirk Aqueduct and watch the canal boats chug slowly by.

Not far from Nesscliffe, we heard about the local legend of Humphrey Kynaston, born 1468, son of Sir Roger Kynaston. Humphrey was a wild and unruly young man who was frequently in trouble with the authorities and a part-time highwayman. Sometimes the king's Men came looking for him. He used to hide in a cave high up in the sandstone cliffs just outside the village, which we used to visit. Today the cave was known as Kynaston's Cave and had an iron door for an entrance. This iron door is said to later have become the door for Shrewsbury gaol. There was also an engraving in the cave, which read "H.K. 1486".

All the time, our baby was growing and could totter around quite happily in our back garden, which was just as

well for I had become pregnant again and was getting tubby around my middle. I was told that my shoulders could have carried a horse.

I was settled and happy in our army quarter, but I did not see a lot of Mike, as he had a very demanding schedule at the camp, training the junior soldiers. He used to come back with lots of amusing tales of what had gone on when he was exercising these young lads. One of the many stories he told me was about a plan hatched up by the young solders when they were told to run around the gym. On his command, "Go," they were all giggling and laughing. Then they ran through the big doors on the side and began running around the outside of the gym. Round and round they ran, thinking it was great fun.

He let them run and run until they started slowing up and were breathing hard. He then lined them up against the side of the gym and told them to get in to the "press-up position." It had been raining hard the night before, and that side of the building was flooded with a large sheet of water coming up to the doors. They protested but had to put their hands into the water and get in to the prone position and start doing the press-ups. "Raise. Lower! Raise. Lower. Raise. Lower. Raise. Lower." Mike was relentless.

The young soldiers were getting tired and got lower and lower as their arms got weaker and weaker. In the end, they were all lying in the puddles totally exhausted and, of course, totally drenched. It would be classed as bullying by today's standard but not then, as discipline was much stricter. The junior soldiers accepted they had been had and squelched away to their next lesson. Needless to say, they did not try that trick again!

One day, Mike came home with the news that we had been allocated a quarter on the camp itself. I received this news with mixed feelings. I was happy where I was, but the new quarter would only be a five-minute bike ride or a fifteen-minute walk away. It was on a corner of English Road at the bottom of the camp, but first we had to "march out" (the army's term for moving out of a quarter) of our house on Nesscliffe. Now march outs were much worse than march in's, and the stories that went with them were legendary.

How to Move out Army Style

The sort of thing the inspecting BIA (barrack inventory accountant) would do was put on white gloves and start checking the cleanliness of the quarter by running his fingers along the skirting boards, the tops of cupboards, and doors, checking for dust. He would make sure the oven was completely free from grease by running his fingers along the undersides of the oven doors. He'd take the inside panels off to check for grease, make sure there were no spots on the trays, check behind and under the oven for grease, and lift the carpet to check underneath to see if they had been wiped clean. (There were no fitted carpets in those days, and no carpets in the bedrooms—just polished brown lino.) The BIA would inspect the pots and pans and make sure they were spotless and check the mattresses for marks or stains. First he would slap the mattress hard to see if a stain or mark had been covered by talcum powder (an old soldier's trick). If a cloud of powder appeared, he would examine the mattress in the closest detail. All damages had to be paid

for, and a mattress was a very expensive item. Scratches on furniture (if not noted on moving in) were property damage and to be paid for. Bedding had to be laundered and clean. Sheets and pillowslips were to be separated into doubles and singles; likewise with the blankets. Curtains were washed and rehung. The three-piece suite would be stripped of covers and laid out on each chair and settee—again to check for marks or stains. Garden tools were cleaned and oiled. Dustbins needed to be free from rubbish and washed clean. The list was endless.

If the quarter was not up to the required standard, it would be refused. The family then had a few days or a week to put right what was required. The shame was that everyone on the estate knew the quarter was not accepted, and the news went around the camp like wildfire. Then the bill for spots, scratches, damages, or items missing was added up, and the amount would be taken from your next month's wages.

It was a lot of hard work and preparation to get the quarter ready. So it was with apprehension that we looked towards the time for our first march out.

It was a bright sunny day, and the BIA arrived promptly at ten o'clock. He started checking the items upstairs first. No white gloves appeared. He checked our bedding and mattresses and seemed satisfied. Then he headed downstairs to the kitchen. All was running smoothly until he came to our mincemeat grinder, which was still in its greaseproof wrapping, laid out on the kitchen table. We had never used it, the horror! There was a tiny rust spot on the part where the minced meat was squeezed through holes in a metal plate. We protested that we had not even taken the

grinder out of its box. But no, it was not acceptable for an incoming occupant, and we had to pay for the new part. The BIA checked the furniture for scratches or marks, but Michael had polished out most of the light scratches that had appeared during our stay.

Then finally it was over. We were no longer the occupants of our house on Nesscliffe. We were a bit upset that we had to pay for an item we had never used. But that was the army system in the '60s. We settled comfortably in our new quarter, and Mike was as busy as ever. Among his many duties, he was put in charge of the Junior Leaders swimming team. Early morning, he would be at the baths training and cajoling the boys to give out their best. This went on for months, but the hard training the team put in resulted in them winning every race in the army junior and senior swimming championships and breaking all existing records that stood at that time. It was a tremendous achievement and accolade for Mike and the Junior Leaders' Regiment.

CHAPTER 14

Baby Anthony and
Back to Jamaica

I was getting bigger and bigger, and my bump kept getting in the way of everything. I had a wonderful midwife looking after me. Every so often, she would turn up to check on my well-being and the progress of my pregnancy. She was definitely "old school", with twenty-five years of midwifery experience behind her. I felt so safe when she was around. She was very brisk and businesslike. I looked upon her as a mother hen. Her name was Nurse Lawrence, and sadly, she's no longer with us.

In October 1965, my back was really aching. I knew I was very near my birth time. I struggled through the day. Nurse Lawrence called in to see how I was coping, and I told her of my discomfort. She said she was going out for a dinner with the family in the evening and, if anything started, I was to let her know immediately. She left the phone number of the restaurant where they were eating.

We were lucky to have a public phone box just across the

road where we lived, as we did not own a phone of our own and mobile phones were only just coming onto the market. Mike had a two-shilling piece (ten pence) put to one side for just such emergencies.

About 10 p.m., the pain was getting much harder, so he rang the restaurant and explained the situation to Nurse Lawrence. Not long after she arrived, Michael was turned out of our bed, and she settled down with me. At 4.50 a.m., our son was born; he was a big healthy eight pounds, two ounces (three kilograms, sixty-nine grams), with the shoulders of a rugby player.

Mike was there at the birth. He said, "It was a very moving experience. So Anthony, our new baby, came in to the world, which was not quite as dramatic as when Aline was born. Some of the headlines of the day ran some version of "The Post Office Tower in London Just Opened". In addition, the police had found a girl's body on a moor near Oldham. The body was quickly identified as that of a little girl who had disappeared just after Christmas at the age of ten. Regular US combat units were deployed in 1965 for the war in Vietnam. Laos and Cambodia were heavily bombed by the United States as the war escalated. The Indonesian government outlawed the Communist Party of Indonesia. All those events seem a world away now.

Our son was exercising his lungs in a very loud and healthy manner. After about two hours of him making his presence known, Nurse Lawrence with all her years of experience, said, "That boy is hungry." She gave him a small bottle of sugar and water.

He went quiet. As soon as it was finished, oh how he yelled for more.

But Nurse Lawrence knew best, and she wrapped him up tightly and settled him down. I wonder if that sort of procedure would be frowned on today.

When the word got around that Anthony had been born, I had many callers. Finally Michael put a note on the front door, saying, "The front door is open. Lilly May is upstairs. Please go up and say hello to her and to our new baby. Mike was tired from going up and down the stairs and busy making tea or coffee for our visitors and arranging flowers in to vases. For a short while, our house rapidly filled with flowers for me and money for our new baby. It was a lovely but exhausting experience.

The excitement of having a new baby soon settled down to a regular routine of boiling nappies, mainly in a galvanised bucket (disposable ones were still very expensive); feeding, changing; preparing meals; and looking after our active two-and-a-half-year-old daughter.

One day, Mike came home saying his time with the Junior Leaders' Regiment was nearly up. He was to be posted back to his own Royal Hampshire Regiment (now disbanded). The regiment was in a transit camp in Hampshire, waiting to be called forward and ready for active service against the Indonesians in Borneo. The Indonesians had made incursions into North Borneo, which at that time was part of Malayan territory. Britain had a treaty with Malaya and was asked to provide troops and to push the Indonesians back to their side of the border.

Oh we were in a dilemma! Where was I to go while he was away in a war zone? Many of the young wives in the regiment had the same problem as me. I remember many

went back home to their parents or to stay with relations. I had visions of ending up in an army hostel again.

Mike and I talked over the situation, and it was decided that I should go back home to Jamaica. That way, if anything happened to him, I would be surrounded by family and places I would be familiar with. First we had to find the money, as he was only on a corporal's wage, which did not stretch very far. We opted to sell our car. The money raised would be a big help towards the fare. It wasn't too long before he found a buyer for our Morris Minor—someone who was a member of the permanent staff at Park Hall Camp. So that was another step forward towards our aim of sending me back home.

CHAPTER 15

Life on Board the SS *Golfito*

We found a ship that was sailing to Jamaica early January 1966, which worked out well as the regiment was due to fly out to Hong Kong in February, with onward transit to Malaya and then later to Borneo. At the beginning of the year, we made arrangements to march out of our quarter, which went off without a hitch or any bills or damages to pay for.

Then Mike had to hire a car and make one more very important journey. He had to take me and our little family down to Southampton Docks to board the SS *Golfito*, which was leaving on 12 January, calling in at Trinidad and then Jamaica. It was a mixture of excitement and sadness when we made the long journey down to Southampton from Oswestry, some 205 miles (329 kilometres). We mostly travelled the main roads, as there were only short stretches of motorways in use then. I was excited that I would be seeing home again yet saddened in the knowledge that I didn't know for how long Mike would be away.

We arrived at the quay where the SS *Golfito* was docked. After a preliminary document check, I was allowed on board. I was shown my cabin, and then I went straight up to the stern of the ship with Aline, carrying Anthony in my arms.

I looked down, and there was Mike—a small lonely figure on the quayside waving a handkerchief. It was a heart-wrenching experience seeing him standing there as the ship slowly pulled away. His outline got smaller and smaller as we disappeared into the mist of the afternoon. Soon the ship was rising and falling with the swell of the outgoing tide. I was crying. Aline was crying. And baby Anthony was crying because his sister and I were weeping nonstop. A reporter wanted to talk me about my trip back to Jamaica and my family, but I was not in a fit state to give an interview to anyone, and sobbing, I made my way back to my cabin and on to my bed.

For me, the crossing across was one of constant seasickness. How I retched and heaved and hardly left my cabin. Luckily, Aline had the ship's nursery to go to every day while I looked after Anthony. I would go to the dining room occasionally or take a walk around the deck, but most of the time was spent in my cabin feeling ill.

There were two young women farther down the corridor who would drop in from time to time, bringing a bottle of Coca Cola or 7 Up, which helped lift my spirits a little.

While on the journey, Anthony needed some treatment from the doctors, and I had to carry him to the surgery several times. And of course, each visit had to be paid for when we finally docked. The cost was six pounds per visit.

In today's money, that works out to ninety-four pounds per appointment.

Oh how I wanted the voyage to end. Every few days, the captain—a cheerless-looking man—would make an appearance while doing an inspection of the ship, accompanied by some of his officers. The times he came to the cabin, he never spoke. He looked around and then disappeared. (It certainly wouldn't be allowed today.)

I thought that, as the weather became warmer and the seas calmer, I would feel less sick. But it wasn't to be. Nearly every day, I would be feeling nauseous. I just wanted the ship to dock. I just wanted to be on dry land again. I just wanted the ship to be still and not rising and falling, no matter how small the swell.

We finally reached Trinidad, and an announcement came over the loudspeaker system that we would be disembarking soon. Oh great! I could get off and walk around on solid earth. As we pulled alongside the berthing area, I gathered up the children and put Anthony in the little buggy I had brought with me and hurriedly strode down the long passageway towards the entrance.

Two ladies were just coming out of their cabin. Both were very elegantly dressed. The older lady turned to me and said, in a most refined and cultured voice, "Excuse me, but are you a service wife?"

I replied that I was, and she complimented me on how well my children were dressed and behaved. We had a long conversation in the corridor with the other lady, who was hovering behind her. I had no idea who she was; I just wanted to get off the ship. I politely excused myself and hurried off towards the exit.

Emerging into the bright sunlight, I saw all the officers lined up in their tropical whites, looking very smart by the gangway. Suddenly the captain stepped forward, looking very angry and shouted, "Madam, will you kindly get that pram out of the way?"

My blood was up. I just wanted to get ashore, and now this miserable-looking man was shouting at me and stopping me. I shouted back at him, "If you want it moved, then *you* move it."

At that point, I thought he was going to burst a blood vessel. He turned to his officers and told them to get me, the children, and the buggy off his deck. Two officers, smothering laughter and giggling, escorted us all down the gangway, complete with the buggy. As we went down the side of the ship, there was a band on the quay who started to strike up some music and then quickly fizzled out as they realised it was only one Jamaican girl, two children, and two officers (who were still giggling) carrying a baby buggy. I heard a tremendous cheer from above, and on looking up, I saw the decks lined with passengers looking down at me all waving, laughing, whistling, and cheering me on. I still didn't understand the significance of it at all. I was so glad to get onto solid ground again. I waved back up to them and carried on towards the town.

Not really knowing where I was to go, I stopped a girl and asked which way the town was. I really needed a hairdresser, as my hair was in a mess. With me feeling so sick, I didn't give it the attention it needed. She was really sweet and volunteered to take me to a salon in the city Port of Spain (the capital). We walked and talked, and she even sat with the children while I had my hair done. I was so

grateful and felt more like my old self when my hair had been washed brushed and tidied up.

Thanking my new friend, I left her and walked around the town with the children, enjoying the hustle and bustle of the place and the hot sun on my shoulders and back. I did a lot of window shopping, and had the pleasurable experience of feeling hard ground beneath my feet.

Eventually, it was time to get back to the ship, ready for our next port of call. On returning, I found I was a minor celebrity due to my rushing off the boat that morning.

People would come up to me and shake my hand or say, "Well done." Unbeknown to me, the lady who I had been talking to in the corridor before I left the ship was Her Royal Highness Princess Alice, Duchess of Gloucester, sister-in-law to Edward VIII and George VII and aunt to Queen Elizabeth II. So she had a very high pedigree. She was also colonel-in-chief to several famous regiments. No wonder she was interested in me as a service wife. The lady who was with her was her lady in waiting and travelling companion. So the realisation dawned on me that I had breached all the rules of protocol and etiquette by not letting HRH off the ship first.

For a day or two afterwards, I was the talking point among all the passengers and crew. And no wonder the captain had been agitated when I upset what must have been his carefully planned disembarking ceremony. The band on the quay that had fallen about laughing was part of the welcoming committee for the princess.

That afternoon, the ship left Trinidad, and soon the island became a hazy outline just along the horizon. It was not long afterwards that old familiar feeling of nausea came back. Once more, I took to my cabin, just wanting to reach

Jamaica, which I found out was some 1,151 miles (1,852 kilometres) north-west of Trinidad. I did miss Mike and wondered how he was coping.

The days slipped by with Aline in the playroom and Anthony with me. Eventually a message came over the speaker system. "Will all passengers kindly clear their accounts and make their way to the forward disembarking point?" Oh great! At last we had arrived. I had to clear my account with the ship's doctor, and I was wondering if I had enough money left.

On calling at his surgery, I was met by his smile. "Mrs Green," he said, "I know you have been suffering with seasickness throughout the voyage. Yet despite your illness, you have been such a good mother to your two children, and your baby boy is so much better. There is no charge."

I was very relieved, and my spirits lifted. Nothing to pay and I had finally reached Jamaica, where I would be on firm and solid ground once more.

CHAPTER 16

My Time at the School

When I disembarked (this time letting HRH Princess Alice off first), the hot Jamaican sun was burning into my shoulders and there on the quayside waiting to greet me was a very good friend, Miss Sawell. I was to stay with her while Mike was away at war. There were lots of hugs and kisses. Then in next to no time, a friend of Miss Sawell's whisked us away to her house on Avondale Avenue, which was in uptown Kingston.

In the car, I was taken back on a nostalgic journey to when Mike and I used to visit the places we now passed. There was the Victoria Craft Market, the biggest one in Kingston. And was next to the docks. Hand in hand, we would stroll down the aisles of the market stalls, with people staring at us, as it wasn't the seen or done thing in those days—a black girl and a white man together. I caught a glimpse of the Salvation Army hall where we were married some five years earlier. Farther on up to Half Way Tree, there on the left, was the Carib Theatre where he met me

for our first date together. Oh how the memories rolled on, and the island seemed so empty without him.

Eventually we arrived at Miss Sawell's large and comfortable house, which she shared with her mother. It was an old colonial building with high ceilings fans, busily stirring the already warm air, and a veranda going the length of the house. Miss Sawell was a teacher, and so in the mornings she would leave to travel on a bus to reach her school. I would help her mother with the household chores, and we got on well with laughs and jokes. The children were happy, Aline playing with me in the garden and Anthony close by in his pram under the shade of a mango tree.

Talking of mangoes, another memory came flooding back to me. When Mike and I were enjoying our engagement party at the house, a huge mango fell from a tree and landed with a crash onto a tray of drinks that were being offered, scattering glasses and drinks everywhere.

I started getting Mike's letters and what a joy to me. They seemed to bring the distance and time so much closer.

About a week after I had settled in, I decided I would visit the place where I used to work—the Salvation Army School for the Blind and Visually Handicapped. I took the journey with the children down to the school. And what a welcome I received. The word had gotten out that I was coming, and in next to no time, I was surrounded by animated cheering and screaming children, all anxious to feel my face, my hair, my legs, and all the parts of me to see how much I had changed. Anthony was whisked away from the excited crowd, over their heads; otherwise he could have been trodden on. Aline, not knowing what to do, clung to my legs until she too was rescued. And the

happy band of children followed me everywhere, asking all sorts of questions until order was restored, and they had to go back to their classes.

Oh it was so lovely to see my dear precious children again. And I was so surprised how they had grown in the three years since I'd left for England. About a month later, Miss Sawell received a phone call from the School for the Blind from Mrs Captain Wicks, asking if I would like to fill in for an officer who had to fly back to the United States, as her mother was very ill.

I was worried about what to do. Where would I put the children? What would Miss Sawell think if I suddenly left her?

We talked it over. Miss Sawell was quite happy for me to take up the offer, and the children would be well looked after by the staff at the school. A week later, with bags packed, I left Miss Sawell's house, and an officer came to collect me. We travelled back down to the school. The welcome was not quite as exuberant as the one I'd received when I had first arrived. But everyone was happy and glad to see me—except the staff who worked in the kitchen.

There was my bitter enemy, Miss Peel, the cook, who for some reason loathed and hated me and had tried everything to stop our wedding and our marriage (as mentioned in my first book). She was still there, along with her "yes, Miss Peel, followers". The situation was made even worse now, for she had to call me Mrs Green so did all the other staff, not just Miss Lilly May as before when I was a young helper working at the school.

I was given the room that had been vacated by the previous officer who had to fly back to the United States. I

quickly settled myself and the children into the place where I was to live for the foreseeable future. My job was to look after the food and ration store and to give out daily amounts to each department. It was a pleasant and easy job, and it left me time to look after my two children.

Aline became a real little mother, taking the children by the hand and leading them to the toilet, to the dining room, or to their dormitories, even though they knew their way themselves. They used to humour her, and she thought she was doing a great job. She was allowed to attend the classes and sit at the back pretending to be at school and listen. Sometimes, she would draw or pretend to read. She was only just over three.

Our son was a lovely happy child and was picked up, swept up in loving arms and carried around the school by anyone who happened to be passing by.

A Mix-Up of Letters

I used to get Mike's letters, and he would let me know how he coping. He left for Borneo a month after I had left. He told me he'd landed in the Persian Gulf for refuelling and then had gone on to Ceylon (now Sri Lanka), stopping off in Hong Kong and then heading up to the New Territories (now handed back to China). There was where he started his fitness training, ready for Malaya and jungle warfare training and patrol along the border at a place called Sha Tau Kok. I used to write to him every night, no matter how tired or sleepy I was. Once the children had been settled, I would sit on the veranda in the cool of the evening and tell him of the day's events.

In his letters, he would tell me of some of the things that he and the other soldiers did while on patrol in the jungle. He told me about a river patrol he was on, when a very large snake was sleeping on a low-hanging branch over the stream they were patrolling. It was low enough for the men to duck under. But no, some bright idiot decided to hit the snake

with his rifle. As he did so, it fell into their boat, hissing and spitting all-round the legs of the soldiers, who by this time were jumping and hopping about like jumping beans, trying to keep out of the way of this very big and enraged serpent, with the boat rocking from side to side. In order to escape from they angry reptile, they all jumped into the muddy brown waters, leaving the boat to chug slowly down the stream. Luckily, it caught in some mangrove roots a bit farther down. They swam up to the boat, to hear the snake knocking and rolling about in the bottom of their craft. One of the soldiers managed to hook his rifle under the snake and heave it over the side. The snake was then swimming in and out between the legs of the soldiers, who were then frantically trying to scramble back into the boat. It was like something out of a comedy film sketch, only it was real.

In another letter, I learned about a time when they thought they were being attacked by the Indonesians in the middle of the night. Outside Mike's tent, there came a very large bang. He and all the other soldiers jumped out of their hammocks, snatching their rifles and thinking, *This is it. We are under attack*, only to find a large wild pig twitching and dying outside of his shelter. The pig had come into the camp probably because it could smell food and was about to go inside Mike's tent when he was spotted and promptly shot by the Iban tracker (a local tribesman who guided the soldiers through the jungle).

Another incident I learned about it in a letter was when Mike and his fellow soldiers were on patrol and looking for a place to settle for the night. The sergeant found what he thought was a good all-round defensive position on a slight

hill—a spot where the jungle was not thick enough to cover a surprise attack from Indonesians.

The Iban tracker said, "No. This is a bad place to be. It is not good. We must go farther away from here."

The sergeant was surprised but followed the tracker's advice and moved 100 yards farther on. During the night, a loud crash came out of the darkness of the jungle. The soldiers quickly took up defensive positions and waited for the forthcoming attack. Nothing happened.

In the morning, when light had filtered down through the trees, they went to see where the noise had come from. It was the first place they were going to bed down the previous night. Termites had eaten away the inside of the trees, which had come crashing down onto the spot where the soldiers would have camped. The Iban's instinct had told him it was a bad place to be. The Iban could read the jungle like we could read a town map.

One day, I received one of Mike's letters. It wasn't the normal sort of "missing-you-like-mad" letter. Rather, it was very terse, angry, and short. "If you cannot be bothered to write, then it is hardly worthwhile carrying on," he wrote.

Oh I was so upset. As I mentioned I had written every night. I took the letter to Mrs Wicks, manager of the school, my dearest and best friend I had ever known, and a very wise woman. She said, "Leave it with me, and I will see what I can do." I don't know how she resolved the issue? Incoming mail was still working, but no overseas mail was going anywhere. So she contacted the British military and asked if a message could be sent out to Corporal Green, who by that time was deep in the jungles of Borneo. It worked!

Mike told me in another letter that he had received a

telegram (forerunner of the email or text) letting him know that there was a postal strike in Jamaica, and when it was over he would get all my letters. Then about ten days later, I had another letter saying all my mail had arrived in one big heap, and he was trying to sort out the date order. I was so relieved and ran to tell Mrs Wicks, who once again had come to my rescue.

He explained that, when the helicopter came with the mail for the soldiers into the jungle clearing, it would hover over the trees. The mailbag would be dropped out the helicopter, which never stayed but just took off in the direction it came. All the men would form a ring around the sergeant or corporal. As the letters were pulled out of the sack, he would call out the name of the soldier to whom the letter was addressed. The soldiers would to go to their bashas (huts or bunks) and read in the privacy of their camp bed, leaving Mike standing alone in the clearing with nothing. He said it was very lonely experience. The men used to tease him, saying, I had run off or found another. It was a very worrying time for him.

After he had received my big pile, he was happy to know that I still loved and missed him very much. Letters play such an important part in a soldier's life; it is his link with home and loved ones when times are hard.

CHAPTER 18

Dedication of Anthony

I had a run-in with the staff, no doubt instigated by Miss Peel, who was saying I was short-changing the rations (soap powder) and giving it to my friend Miss Sawell. I was furious and went again to Mrs Wicks. She demanded an instant locker search of all the staff. The soap powder was found, along with other items, hidden in a locker by one of the staff. She was dismissed on the spot, told to clear her things and leave the school immediately.

After that, there were no more complaints or accusations from Mrs Peel and kitchen staff. But they were always cold and surly towards me, not that I was bothered as I had very little to do with them, except when I had to issue rations.

In April of that year, I wanted my son to be "dedicated" (the Salvation Army term for a christening). Thomas, Captain and Mrs Wicks' son, wanted to be part of the ceremony. Now Thomas was a bit of a rebel going through his teenage years, causing lots of heartache to his mum and dad. He had long hair, which he refused to comb, and no

amount of telling him to get it cut helped. Any such pleas would simply fall on deaf ears.

He really wanted to be at our baby's dedication. But I said, "Thomas, I would love you to be his godfather, but with hair like that, I'm afraid it won't be acceptable. The days went by, but no! Thomas continued to sport his unruly thatch on his head.

It was the day before the dedication when a clean-shaven and well-groomed young man came walking down the pathway to my quarters. I hardly recognised him; the wild unkempt teenage rebel of a week ago had made this tremendous change to become a smart and clean-looking young adult. He had a grin as wide as Montego Bay and said he would love to be Anthony's godfather and had even brought a small silver cup engraved with his name for the ceremony.

The dedication was a great success, with a very proud looking Thomas holding Anthony, and two very pleased parents looking on. Captain and Mrs Wicks had gotten their son back to a recognisable human being once again. (I still have photographs of that memorable day.)

Back Home to England

The months passed slowly by. I settled into a routine of issuing stores, looking after my children, and spending time with Captain and Mrs Wicks and Miss Sawell as the hot lazy days merged into one another. And always, there was that still deep ache of missing Mike.

One day, a letter came from him, saying their time in Borneo was nearly up, as the Indonesian president had been overthrown, and a new one was in place. A pact of peace was made between Malaya and Indonesia and the fighting ceased. The regiment was to leave as soon as possible. So I had to make arrangements to get back to England.

Once again, Captain and Mrs Wicks came to my aid by looking around to find the best way to get home. It was decided that the cheapest way was by cargo ship. I was not at all happy, as I had suffered from seasickness on the long voyage out and I certainly didn't want the same feeling going back. But as money was tight, I had to accept that form of getting back to England. (Airfares were still very

expensive then.) I was booked to sail in November '66 on the SS *Northern Lights*, a steamer carrying bananas between Jamaica and England.

When I told Aline, she was delighted that she would be seeing her daddy again. To Anthony, the picture of Michael on my bedside locker was called Daddy, so he saw his "daddy" every day.

In October, I had a letter from Mike. He would be flying back to England, arriving on the fifteenth. After two weeks leave, he was to be based in Wiltshire. I was not to come back yet, as he had the problem of finding an army quarter for us. As before, he didn't qualify with enough points to be allocated a quarter—the reason being the three years he was away from the regiment serving at the Junior Leaders' Regiment in Oswestry. Being a soldier's wife certainly had its problems.

October merged into November. News came from him that, as a short-term measure, he had hired another caravan just outside the village Netherhavon, and I was to come as soon as possible.

When the time came, my mind was in turmoil. I would not be seeing my lovely blind girls again. I had so many mixed emotions. I would miss the long hot tropical days of a Jamaican climate and the noise of the colourful birds and insects. I would miss the rush and buzz of people going about their business and the tall palm trees that were everywhere and swayed in the warm breezes. And I would be back in the cold climate of England. Yet I was excited at the thought of seeing my husband again.

It was a tearful goodbye to all my friends as I reluctantly boarded the SS *Northern Lights* in Kingston Harbour.

To my surprise the captain greeted me personally and told me that I was the only passenger. The plus side was that I had a suite of rooms all to myself. The voyage back to the United Kingdom was quite different from my outward journey. The crew was friendly and whisked both children away and looked after them so well I hardly saw them during the day. They had great fun and had the run of the entire run ship, except for the engine room. I dined with the captain nearly every night, and I looked upon him as a father figure. He was a very polite and distinguished gentleman. Occasionally, I would feel nauseous, and the captain would order one of his crew to get out a deckchair, place it down on the sheltered side of the ship, and settle me on it. Then the crew member would cover me with a blanket, and the fresh air and blue sea seemed to relax me.

As we travelled further north, the seas turned from blue to grey, and the skies overhead became dull and leaden. It was a sure sign that we were not far from England. It was 6 December when we finally docked, and from the deck looking down onto the rainy and windswept quayside was my Mike, waving and smiling for the entire world to see.

Aline was overjoyed at seeing her daddy once again, giving him lots of hugs and kisses when we disembarked, while our son took one look at him and ran off. To him, the picture on my bedside locker was Daddy, not this strange-looking man who he knew nothing about. (He had been only two and a half months old when Mike had left for Borneo.) I had to run after him and caught him just before he got to the edge of the quayside and would have fallen in.

I'd said my goodbyes to the captain and many of the crew. They were all sorry to see me go, for I had made good

friends while on board. They said they would really miss the children.

The journey up to Netherhaven was uneventful, except I had to sit in the back with Anthony, as he was still unsure of his father. While Aline had the front seat and chattered away quite happily with her dad. I was not looking forward to our new temporary accommodation, as memories of our last caravan came flooding back—recollections of the unhappy times of morning sickness that lasted well into the afternoon and the loneliness I had endured.

When we arrived, I was pleasantly surprised. The caravan was newer, bigger, and more modern than the previous one, and I knew it would not be before long we would have an army quarter, as Mike had already been told he was high on the waiting list.

The routine was the same, though. He would leave in the morning for airfield camp, and I was then on my own to look after the children and the household chores. I used to look forward to the evenings when he would return, usually telling me about the day's events.

One evening, we were all at home when there was a commotion outside, lots of running feet, and shouting. Mike looked out of the window and, to his horror, saw a caravan well and truly ablaze opposite ours. He dashed out to see if he could help, but it was all in hand with others who were there. The fire brigade was on its way, and there was nobody inside. The heat was tremendous, and in no time the caravan was reduced to a burning shell.

The whole incident seemed to last about ten minutes. And when the fire brigade did arrive, all they could do was damp down the smouldering remains of the bent

and twisted framework of the caravan. The rest had been completely destroyed, but the people and baby who lived there were safe.

Not long after that incident, Mike came home with a big grin and said, "Get packing!

We have been allocated a quarter in Tidworth," which was on the edge of Salisbury Plain and was then the training ground of the British Army.

CHAPTER 20

On the Move Again

Living in a caravan, there was not much to pack. The day came when we travelled to our new quarter, which was on an army estate. The BIA was there to meet us, and we went through the army procedure of marching in. By now, we were becoming veterans of marching in and out.

Our quarter was at the end of a road with nothing to stop the chilling winds that swept off Salisbury Plain, so the house, although big, was always cold. Our neighbours were nice, and next door were two pretty young girls of Turkish origin, who loved to pass the time with me. Their dad had very strong principles and was always in trouble with the military authorities. More than once, the military police called to take him off to the army jail because he had refused some order.

On the other side was a couple whose wife seemed full of envy. If someone had bought something new she would want one of whatever it was. Michael was sent to Aldershot on his advanced army physical training course. She kept on to her

husband, Jim, moaning and complaining and saying that he should be bettering himself and getting away on more courses. He worked in the stores issuing and collecting army kit. Poor man, he was always very quiet, almost invisible. (The soldiers had nicknamed him "Action Man".)

Now the course Mike was on was very important, as it was a stepping stone into the Royal Army Physical Training Corps. But the drawback was, it lasted for three months and was very intense. He joined with a group of twenty-nine others, all competing for about twelve places. He was posted down to the Army Physical Training School in Aldershot and could only get home at the weekends. He would come home physically tired, as the demands on his body were extreme. He had to excel in all the major sports the army trained soldiers for, which included battle training, endurance runs, combat training, football, swimming, basketball, boxing, and athletics. In addition, there were other sports, such as gymnastics, hockey, cross-country running, and more. But he had to get high marks on those major events.

My life at the married quarter settled into a routine, and I made some good friends. I found Aline a little nursery so she could play with children of her own age, while Anthony was quite content to be with me.

Good news came through from my husband. He had passed all the qualifications required to get into the corps and, at the same time, made a little bit of history, as he was the oldest soldier ever to be accepted into the Royal Army Physical Training Corps at the age of nearly thirty, when all the others were in their early twenties. Once more, the army was about to move us.

Life at the Royal Military Academy Sandhurst

Mike had been posted to the Royal Military Academy at Sandhurst, which was an elite posting, and only those instructors who were handpicked could get there. It was there that they trained the officer cadets until they passed all the skills to become leaders of men under their command in all known military and extreme situations. The course for them was three years, which later changed to terms and probably has changed again. So another posting and another march out, and we were off to Camberley in Surrey.

We still had the problem of finding a place to live, as the married quarters where we were going to be housed were still being built. We managed to find a flat in a place called Yately, not too far from the academy (as it was known). It was over a chemist shop in a little shopping plaza. At the end of the row of flats and underneath, there was a fish and chip shop, which came in quite handy. More than once, people knocked on our door sometimes at night, asking if we could

open the chemist shop so they could get headache tablets or pills for their stomach or other medicines. Of course we told them that we only lived in the flat, and the man who ran the shop lived elsewhere.

We soon settled into our little apartment. Our children were growing, and Anthony played quite happily with the little boy whose father ran the fish and chip shop.

It was during that time we decided to have a holiday with the children. We chose a place in the south of England. It was Holiday Camp in Devon. There was (to the children) a long car journey with the usual choruses from the back seat. "Are we there yet?" The children were all excited and wanting to out and go on all the slides, swings, and other attractions they could see as we checked in to the camp and were given the key to our chalet. Now we could spend a proper family holiday together. It was a lively and happy place, and there were competitions and games and dancing every night.

Under protest, I entered the contest for the Miss Queen of the Week and was voted in, against eleven other girls, with loud clapping and cheering. Mike entered for the King of the Week and won. Aline became runner-up princess of the week, and Anthony was voted in as prince of the week. The compère said he had never seen a family sweep the board, and we must be very unusual.

The next day I was asked to pose for a photo in the local paper. I was asked to shorten my dress, so it was above the knees, I had the winner's tiara on my head and a big sash across my body saying, "Miss Seaton Holiday Winner." I was really self-conscience. Those were the days of the miniskirt. And I was seated on top of children's merry-go-round

showing lots of leg. Lots of photos were taken, and I still have a framed picture on our wall as my claim to fame.

Not long after that, a letter came, asking if I would like to enter the *Daily Mirror* (newspaper) competition for the "Miss Young Britain Award". I explained I had two young children to look after and never heard any more from them.

It was a time when you could leave your young children sleeping in your chalet. The system was, if you tied a handkerchief on the door handle, the patrol going round knew that children were inside. If they heard a child cry, they would inform the entertainments staff over the PA system, who would announce that there was a child crying in whatever chalet they were in. The mother or father would go back to their cabin and see to the child. It worked! It was such a simple arrangement but very effective. Sadly those days have long gone.

It was not too long when news came through that we were due to take over our army quarter on the academy grounds. So it was another march in. Everything was new— the carpets, the furniture, the bed linen, the blankets, the utensils. The cutlery was still wrapped in greaseproof paper. The new cooker was bright and gleaming, with not a spot of grease on its oven liners anywhere. The garden tools were oiled and ready to use. We even had an upstairs carpet in the main bedroom, a luxury in those days.

Life at the academy was very active, and we had a very full social life. Nearly every month, there was a dinner and dance or cheese and wine party, mixed in with full military mess functions and the occasional "ladies night". This was where the men all waited on the ladies. We swept in to the sergeants' mess wearing our ballgowns or our flowing long

dresses to be seated at the long tables. The men were all dressed in their full mess uniforms and then they served and waited on us ladies. We felt like royalty, and the food was usually delicious. All these functions were classified as being "on duty". So even if Mike did not attend, he was still charged at the end of the month on his "mess bill".

We had so many social functions to attend it was hard keeping up with what to wear, and it was also proving very expensive. The wives ended up swapping gowns and dresses among one another. Babysitting was another problem, but we somehow always managed to find a reliable person to sit until we returned.

I remember my very first mess dinner night. I wore a long blue beautiful slinky silky dress, with a silver handbag and silver shoes to match. A glittering pendant hung around my neck. I felt a real lady. I was very nervous as Mike and I walked in to the sergeants' mess with all eyes upon us. I was the first black lady to attend one of these functions. I need not have worried, for I was instantly accepted. The men and other wives were friendly and courteous. This was how it was throughout our stay at the academy.

Michael was busy training the officer cadets, who were very polite and usually very well educated. Their main drawback, though, was they seemed to lack good old-fashioned "common sense". He was under instruction to train the cadets very hard in the first year, to see if they would crack or break under the physical strain. Very few did, and a good rapport was built up between the cadets and instructors. There were many fun incidents between them.

At the end of each term it was "customary" to throw the instructor into the lake at the bottom of the academy

grounds. One of the instructors got fed up with this custom, as it was December and was very cold. He took his cadets to the training ground at the top of the academy, where it was high and there was not a drop of water to be seen, except for a few puddles. The cadets soon saw the situation and shouted, "Staff, you are going the wrong way."

Ignoring their shouts, the instructor kept doggedly on, running them deeper and deeper into the training ground.

Realising they were going to be deprived of their only chance of throwing him into the lake, they jumped on him. They stripped off his clothes except for his socks and boots and then scattered in all directions back down to their living quarters—leaving a very cold, pink, naked, and shivering instructor to make his way down to the gym, dodging from building to building and trying to keep out of sight.

Another standing joke among the instructors was when they were taking the young cadets on athletics and field events. They were told, "If you walk in front of the javelin area and get speared by one, lie still until we can measure the throw, just in case it becomes an academy record." The cadets used to stare at them and wonder if it was true!

At the academy, there were many princes, mainly from the Middle East. One evening at an academy boxing match, the permanent staff and families could attend. We pointed out to Aline that sitting in front of us were two princes. She, in a very loud and demanding voice, said, "Where are the crowns for their heads?" causing the princes to turn round and smile.

Another time, a prince asked Mike if he could see him in his room after the training for the day had finished. He duly turned up, wondering what the prince wanted him for. It turned out that he was offering him a job in his

father's army as an instructor. The pay and conditions were very good, and the whole package sounded quite attractive. He talked it over with me, and after a long discussion, we decided not to take the offer. If we had, our lives would have taken a whole new direction.

At that time, I was heavily pregnant, making Mike being sent on a parachute course at RAF Abingdon in Oxfordshire even worse than it would have been otherwise. I had the double worry of him throwing himself out of a plane and the imminent birth of our baby.

It was at the academy that Marie, our youngest daughter, was born—at Aldershot Cambridge Military Hospital in April 1971 (which closed its doors for the last time in 1996). That year, she was born into headline incidents such as 500,000 people marching on Washington in protest against the Vietnam War; a Tsunami rising to eighty-five metres in height over the Ryukyu Islands (Japan) and throwing a 750-ton block of coral 2.5 kilometres inland; and the beginning of a major eruption of Mount Etna in Sicily, which seriously threatened several small villages on Etna's east flank.

A few months later was Marie christening. In fact, she had two! One was in the morning at the Salvation Army Hall in Aldershot. The Salvation Army officers there were members of The Joystrings, a song group who were famous in the '60s and '70s. The other was in the afternoon at the Royal Chapel in Sandhurst, and that was taken by the Chaplain General Reverend John Millett, who was chaplain general to all of the British Army.

So Marie should have been a saint, having had a double christening. But her nature has turned out to be "happily cheeky", rather than saintly!

CHAPTER 22

A Quick Dash Home and Back

One day, Mike came home with a big smile on his face and said, "Get your bags packed. We are off to Jamaica." He had managed to get an "indulgence flight". That was when the RAF flew a military or specialised flight on which spare seats were available and offered them to any members of the armed forces. It was very quick; he told me on the Thursday, and by Sunday, the entire family was travelling down to Brize Norton to pick up the plane.

It turned out to be a training run for take-offs and landings for the queen when she was travelling around the Caribbean. It was the queen's personal aircraft (a Comet), so although we didn't travel first class, it was still a small claim to fame to be flying in her plane. Mike managed to get some leave, and so we were off with seventeen others.

Landing in the Azores, we flew from there on to Bermuda and then to Nassau, Antigua, and on to Jamaica. It was a great shock to my uncle when we turned up, as he'd

only found out hours before that we would be arriving, even though we had sent a telegram the Thursday we knew we could fly. It turned out there was another cable and wireless strike on the island, and there were no details of flights or information was being sent out. We realised that we would not get any information when the plane returned from its onward journey. So we decided we had better play it safe and come back the next day, as the plane was still on the runway. The aircrew were surprised to see us when we arrived, but soon we took off and headed towards Barbados and finally headed for home.

It took us about a week to do the travelling, and in that time, we had travelled some 9,500 miles. And it only cost us as a family £40 return (£7,700 at 2016 prices!). I don't think that will ever happen again. Life at the academy was pleasant with the three children—Aline at school and Anthony was looked after by a friend and Marie in her pram. I managed to get a part-time job in the National Army Museum, then housed in the academy and full of fascinating and interesting objects. I used to clean the Duke of Wellington's uniform and the saddle of his horse called Copenhagen. There was Florence Nightingale's lamp. There were beautifully engraved swords, muskets, pistols uniforms maps, and other military equipment on display.

CHAPTER 23

A Miserable Time

Mike had to go away from time to time, either to France or Germany on exercise with the cadets. But on most occasions, I saw him every night. The months slipped into years, and then the time came when he had his next posting. This time it was to the Queens Lancashire Regiment in Germany, which was a modern university town in the north-west of Germany. We had the same problem as before. There was not a quarter available for us. Mike had to leave me and the children while he joined the regiment.

For a while, I went to stay with Mike's sister Jeanne and her husband Johnny in Winchester. Together, ran a small cafe at the bottom of the city, very near the statue of King Alfred and Winchester Cathedral. It was a very busy place, as many tourists used to drop in there for a cup of tea or coffee.

Unfortunately, staying there did not work out very well. Jeanne, at the time, was suffering from nerves and used to follow the children around picking on every little fault that

occurred, which made our two older children very unhappy. Marie was still a baby, so it didn't affect her. It also upset me, and I desperately wanted to get away. But where was I to go?

I used to go for long walks in the park or around the cathedral grounds pushing the pram and with the two older children. I just wanted to get away. For a while, I helped in the cafe or helped in the kitchen. But Jeanne would criticise whatever it was I was doing.

Some weeks later, I was invited back to Sandhurst to visit friends and stay for a few days. They were shocked to see how drawn and thin I looked and how unhappy the children were. I explained the situation and how it was for us all. They kindly offered to put us up until Mike was allocated a quarter in Osnabruck and when I could go to Germany and be with him. I was so grateful for this chance.

So it was a trip back down to Winchester to collect our belongings and then back up to Sandhurst. I think Jeanne was relieved we had found somewhere else to stay, and it took us a long time to heal the rift that had developed between us.

My friends Joyce and Wesley were a lovely couple, and the children were soon back to being their happy bouncy selves. I was once more feeling relaxed, except for the lonely ache of missing my husband. He was, by this time, doing a tour of duty in Belfast, staying in a place called Flax Street Mill. It was a long brick building leading right down to the edge of the Ardoyne and a stronghold of the hard line Irish Republican Army (IRA). Occasionally, they were targeted by snipers, who hid out in the spire of the Holy Cross Church nearby. They had to patrol the streets and keep a lookout for the trouble spots. They did several raids

on known IRA sympathisers, which were always fraught with danger, as the people in the street would turn on all the lights in their houses, bang on dustbin lids, and generally form a crowd to impede the soldiers.

CHAPTER 24

Another Army Quarter

One day I had an official letter saying my husband had been allocated an army house in Osnabruck, and I was to fly out from RAF Brize Norton to RAF Gutersloh, where a duty driver would be there to pick me and the family up and take us to our quarter in Osnabruck. The day came when I had to say goodbye to my friends, and Wesley drove me down to Wiltshire to catch my plane. I was so grateful for their kindness, putting me up during the difficult time I had spent at Michael's sister, and it was with sorrow in my heart that I had to say farewell to them both.

I arrived in Gutersloh (northern Germany), and sure enough, there was a driver waiting to take us on to Kastanien Strasse (Chestnut Street in English). The first few miles with the driver, I was terrified, as we were driving on the wrong side of the road. It took me a little time to realise that we were now on the continent, and the rule of the road was to drive on the right. We arrived at the quarter just as it was getting dark.

The family officer was there to see me in, and the BIA (now changed to ASA; same job, different title!) would meet me in the morning. The children had great fun chasing through the house and exploring all the rooms, from the large attic in the roof to the cellar where the coke boiler was housed.

I put Marie down so she could crawl around, and to my horror, the baby romper suit she was in turned grey. What I had thought was a grey carpet was indeed a light blue but was so full of dust it looked grey! Not a good start to my new home. I had to put the children upstairs while I got on my hands and knees and scrubbed the carpet back to its original colour.

The ASA did arrive the next day, and we went through the army routine of marching in. I told him about the state of the carpet. He was very apologetic, but there was nothing he could do; the previous occupants had left some time before, and the quarter had been empty for some time.

Another fault was the pile of coke in the cellar. This was to fuel the central heating of the house. The former occupants had left a big pile of clinker (burnt and worthless coke) and carefully placed the proper coke on top of the pile, making it look as if there was a large quantity of unused coke waiting to be burnt. This had to be paid for month by month, so the ASA had to do a rapid recalculation and work out a refund on our fuel bill and then order some more. So we had both been cheated.

I soon settled in to our house in Kastanien Strasse and quickly made friends with our neighbours either side. Aline had a girl to play with, who was a little older than her, while

Anthony, who didn't go out very often, had a boy who he occasionally met up with.

There were arrangements made for the wives whose husbands were in Ireland to link up by telephone, and we were allotted three minutes to talk to our loved one. Through one of these calls, I found out that Mike was due for R&R (rest and recuperation) and would be back with me soon. It made the waiting and longing seem even deeper.

One evening there was a knock at the door, and I wondered who that could be. I looked out of the kitchen window, and to my delight, it was him. I rushed out and flung my arms around his neck and kissed him with a deep and wonderful feeling. He laughingly told me that he hadn't been sure if it was the right house. When I had moved to Germany, he had been in Ireland, and all he had was the address. He'd had to get the duty driver to bring him to Kastanien Strasse.

Oh joy! He was home for four days, and there was so much I had to tell him. He woke up the children, who were very excited to see him. There were lots of hugs and kisses and sweets and presents to give out. It was a real welcome home time.

But the days passed so quickly, and all the jokes, laughter, and feelings of togetherness disappeared in a moment of time. He was gone, leaving just a faint smell of aftershave on a pillow or a small pile of socks and shirts to wash and put away.

Life soon settled down again—to looking after all three children and the general running of the house.

It was March when the regiment came back from Ireland and soon settled in to soldiering by going on exercise in the

various training grounds around Germany. Sennelager and Hohne seemed to be the favourite training areas. Mike was back in the gym and training the boxing team, refereeing volleyball matches, taking the men out on endurance runs, and generally keeping the regiment's fitness levels up to standard. It was lovely to have him back and be together as a family again.

It didn't last, for he was off to Canada to do adventurous training in the Rockies. So I was back to bringing up and looking after the children. I managed to get a job, which worked out well, as Aline and Anthony were off to school, and Marie was at nursery school. The work involved looking after and tidying the rooms of the teachers' accommodation quarters, which were just across the road from where we lived. It wasn't too strenuous, but the state of some of the rooms was quite untidy. It made us cleaners wonder if the teachers behaved like that when they were at home. They taught the British children in various schools around the Osnabruck area. They were given officer status, so they had staff to clean their quarters.

I made good friends with one of the ladies who lived opposite our house, and we shared many a joke and a laugh between us. One day, she seemed upset. I could sense she wanted to talk. It appeared that one of the teachers had made complaints about her, saying her room was not up to the standard expected and that my friend was too slow in doing her job. So the supervisor in charge of the quarters had put her on a warning. We were angry! Here was a jumped-up 25- to 30-year-old telling my friend, a mature and conscientious woman who had a husband and two children and had moved in and out of many army quarters,

how the room should be cleaned. What's more, the woman was going round putting talcum powder down the sides of her settee or pieces of paper under a cushion to catch my friend out. I agreed that when I had finished my rooms, I would come and check hers just to make sure there were no more sneaky tricks she had thought up or ways to catch her out.

Not long after that incident, I had a letter from Mike that was full of his adventures in Canada.

CHAPTER 25

Canada

At first, Mike had been staying at a place called Medicine Hat—a training ground of the British Army then on the edge of Banff National Park in the Rockies. He'd canoed down the Saskatchewan River (Indian for fast-flowing) exploring the mountains around Banff. He'd climbed an unnamed mountain peak to 10,000 feet (3,048 metres); they'd called it Hoggies Back after Captain Hoggie, the Officer who was in charge of the adventure training unit. Mike and the captain were caught in an electrical storm at the top of a mountain, with rocks cracking all around them as they were being positively charged, and then narrowly missing a lightning strike as they ran off the peak. He'd climbed the Athabasca Glacier and practiced ice and crevice techniques, among all sorts of other activities the soldiers had to carry out. It was exciting for Mike, but it certainly wasn't exciting for me. He'd even had a run-in with a bear that had come to investigate the camp they were in. All the soldiers had gone back to the training unit. So he was alone

for two days. The camp was quiet—and completely isolated. As the winter weather was closing in a family of bears was showing a great interest in the tents and the dustbins at the edge of the camp. Soon the bear became more and more bold and was wandering among the tents. The only thing Mike had to drive the animal away was firecrackers given to him by a Canadian Ranger, which popped and banged and jumped all over the place.

After a day of this, he was fast running out of crackers. The bear was clawing and tearing the nearby tents because it could smell food. He woke on the second morning to find the bear staring at him from about five metres away. He had no rifle or anything to defend himself, so he dived back in his tent, picked up an orange, and hurled it at the bear. It bounced off the bear's head, and with a grunt, the bear padded off to the edge of the camp.

Later in the afternoon the second set of soldiers arrived and the bear made off to the edge of the trees because it was unsure of all the noise and hustle that camp life brings.

To me, it sounded horrible and very dangerous. What if he had been drowned in the river or been hit by lightning on top of the mountain or fallen into a crevice on the glacier? Or suppose the bear had attacked him? It was times like this when I really did miss him.

Six weeks later, he was back and looking very fit and very brown and had even grown a moustache. Aline, who was running towards him, shouting, "Daddy, Daddy," took one look at him, burst in to tears, and refused to hug or kiss him until he had shaved it off!! Life returned back to normal—well, as normal as possible being an army wife.

CHAPTER 26

A Very Smart New Car

One day we were out and passed a garage, which had, among other cars, a beautiful Opel Commodore. It was a rich deep orangey red and was a demonstration model in perfect condition, with not many miles on the clock. The dashboard looked like a plane cockpit full of dials and gauges. The upholstery was jet-black in colour and very comfortable, and the engine had the purr of a contented cat. Now our existing car was a rather battered BMW and was held together with "prayers and chewing gum".

I had already been picked up for speeding by the police as we were on our way to Verden, where Mike had to referee a water polo match. A man walked out in to the middle of the road, holding up what I thought was a lollipop. We screeched to a halt, and I was about to shout at him for walking into the road, when Mike said, "Oh no. It's the police."

The man gestured me to wind down the window and started to say something to me.

Mike quickly replied, "Es tut mir sehr leid dass wir keine deutsch sprechen" (I'm sorry; we do not speak much German).

So he replied in perfect English, "You were travelling at 110 kilometres an hour in an 80-kilometre zone and have been picked up by our radar van." And he proceeded to tell me off for speeding and also Mike for not supervising me enough, as I was still on L-plates.

I started arguing, but Mike was saying quietly but urgently, "Shut up! Never argue with the German police." He was worried about what might have happened if the policeman had looked closely at our car. He would have seen tyres that were worn and borderline and bodywork was more rust than metal. The suspension had a definite lean to the left, which had to be compensated by continually steering to the right. The engine and brakes were good, but that was about all. The upshot of it was I had a thirty-five-mark fine on the spot (this was before the euro), and I only had a fifty-mark note, so I was left with fifteen marks, I was not happy! But Michael was, as the polizei (German police) had not looked too hard at our elderly BMW.

On our way back from Verden, we called in at the garage where we had seen the Opel Commodore and asked how much the place would give for our present car? The mechanics put it on their ramp and seemed to take ages inspecting it. Again, we were worried because we thought the inspection would come at a big cost. When finished, the inspectors said the engine was very good, but "das Auto ist Müll" (the bodywork is rubbish). However, as the car we liked was a demonstration model and had been used, they could sell it to us at cost. It was a price we could just afford,

and so a few days later, we were the proud owners of this stunning-looking car, which definitely turned heads as we drove by.

I also passed my driving test in Osnabruck. It was called a "tick test" for the questions and then a practical driving test around the town. The testing was through the military. And several times, I was ready to sit the test and drive with a military instructor, only to be put back because of some army commitment elsewhere. I was becoming a "bag of nerves".

One day, I was told an instructor was being posted into the regiment, and I could go with him. I took the tick test, asking the instructor what he would do in such-and-such a situation and quickly writing down the correct answers he unknowingly gave me. That was the first hurdle over.

Then I had to take the practical test around the town. As he was new to the district, he just said, "Take me for a drive around the area." So I took him around the routes I knew well.

When I had finished, he said, "You are a good driver, but you are so nervous I would like to take you again next week when you have settled down a bit. I haven't failed you but just want reassure myself that you are the competent person I think you are."

The rest of the week seemed to go on forever, dragging slowly by. Finally, the test day arrived. Was I ready? With my heart pounding and giving my instructor my very best smile, I took the driving seat, and off around the town we went. This time it was a pass. I could now legally drive our beautiful car. Oh! I could have kissed the instructor. But I didn't.

Mike did not get much use of the car, as he had another tour of Northern Ireland. Again it was Belfast but in a different area and in another mill—this time in Albert Street but in a slightly quieter location. Normally, the PT instructor was designated as the commanding officer's bodyguard and went with him everywhere. But this CO had his own preference, which was not Mike. So he was put in charge of the rest and recuperation programme, as well as keeping the men as fit as possible and organising youth club activities for the local youngsters.

He even organised an abseiling course down one of the lift shafts of the mill. During the day, he was in an office arranging for the soldiers four days R&R leave back to the United Kingdom, organising indoor games for the men and running a youth club in the evenings. In addition, he met the men on their return from R&R at Aldergrove Airport (now known as Belfast International Airport), sometimes in the early hours of the morning.

There were times when it could be dangerous when he was at the airport or at the youth club, which was only a few streets away from the mill, as he would not be armed. Normally he, like all the soldiers, carried his rifle everywhere. When on youth club duties, he had a bodyguard with him, carrying a Browning pistol in his inside pocket, while Mike was running around in a tracksuit with the youngsters. He said that, without his rifle, he felt completely naked.

The regiment's first casualty while they were on their tour of duty was a soldier who went to the toilet. He pulled the chain, and the rusty cistern brackets broke off the wall. The cistern fell on his head, knocking him out!

CHAPTER 27

The Crunch

I used to drive up to the wives club for a cup of tea and talk to the other wives. By this time, we had a garage farther up the road. It was in a row of garages, but nobody wanted the end garage, because all the dustbins would be parked outside it. Despite a very big notice asking for the bins to be kept clear of that area, no one ever did.

One day, I was in a hurry to get to the wives club because Mike was due to ring me from Ireland. Sure enough, all the dustbins were scattered in front of our garage. I was so mad. I had to struggle to get the heavy bins to one side to open the garage door. Fuming, I jumped in the car; reversed out; and, in doing so, caught the wing, which made a terrible metallic scraping sound along the wall of the garage. Horrified, I jumped out. There down the left side was a huge scrape mark that ran down the side of the car. Oh No! What was Mike going to say?

I drove up to the wives club nervous and not looking forward to the phone call and in shock. I told most of the

wives, and they went out and had a look at the damage and were sorry for me.

Eventually, the phone rang, and it was my turn to take the call. Mike sounded bright and cheerful and asked if I was all right, as I didn't sound my usual self. I told him about the car and the big scrape down the side. What he said made me feel so much better. He said, "May providing you are all right, that's all that matters. We can get another car, but I can't get another May." That lifted my spirits, and our call was soon at an end.

Some of the wives gathered round, asking, "What did he say?" I told them what he'd said about getting another car and not being able to replace me, and they were amazed, saying, "Huh, my husband would have shouted and sworn at me." I was so thankful to have a man like Mike. One of the wives told me where I could get our car fixed, and the next day, despite a sleepless night, I was up early to get to the garage / body shop.

The man in charge said, "Ya, we can make your car look good again. Come back this afternoon, and it will be ready."

The day passed slowly, and at three o'clock, I went back to find our car looking as if nothing had happened to the wing and as sleek as ever. I need not have told Mike, as it was back to its striking lines again, and I was so pleased.

He was halfway through his tour of duty with the Queens Lancashire Regiment and was thinking ahead to when we returned to England. We decided that we would buy a new car—this time, a right-hand drive that was brand new. He spent many nights looking through brochures of different makes, weighing up the good and bad points of each. We eventually settled on a Volkswagen Golf, a fast

nippy economical five-door hatchback. If only we could afford another new Opel Commodore. But the price range was out of our reach.

We had a good trade-in price for our much-loved Opel, and Mike ordered our new one. As it was a right-hand drive model, it had to come from the main factory in Wolfsburg, in northern Germany.

Eventually, it arrived, and we were the proud owners of our gleaming shiny new Volkswagen. We had never owned a new car before, so it was especially exciting to sit behind the wheel and take in that special smell that only a new car can bring.

The children were not impressed, as they were used to the much bigger Opel with more room in the back.

The four-month tour of duty in Northern Ireland passed by, and Mike was back catching up on all the news and being a husband again.

Holiday in Italy

In September of 1974, Mike had a chance to book a holiday in Italy, as there were army caravans for hire near Lido di Jesolo, a resort across the bay from Venice. We thought it would be a good chance to show the children another part of Europe and, of course, the famous waterways and canals of Venice.

The day eventually arrived when our new car was well packed with everything, including a ten-day army rations pack (you could buy the packs in those days). And we were off for seven days. The children at first were all excited, but the novelty soon wore off and the familiar cries from the back came: "Are we there yet?"

It was a very long journey, taking us some 1.189 kilometre (740 miles) distance, with stops in between as we travelled down the south of Germany through Austria and into Italy. I was driving some of the time, but found I was hallucinating and wandering over the road. I had taken some travel-sick tablets, and I just couldn't seem to

concentrate. So Mike had to take over. So it was some very sleepy children and I, feeling like a zombie, plus a very tired driver finally reached our destination some thirteen hours later.

The caravan park was a mixture of English and Germans set out in two lines. On one side were the German caravans, looking all pristine and very modern, while the English caravans were looking rather dated and tired. No matter! For us, it was an inexpensive holiday, where we could be together as a family. We had a lovely time at Lido di Jesolo and saw Venice and the little islands of Murano and Burano, famous for its glass and lacemaking. The sun was very hot, and once on the beach, we had to race across burning sand to get our feet into the cool waters of the lagoon.

At the caravan park, the Germans and English kept much to their separate lines, with the occasional "Guten Tag" (Good day) from the Germans or a "hello" from our side.

The evening before we were due to drive back, we were packing our belongings and Mike had mislaid the car keys and had to unpack and go through everything he had carefully put away into our cases. This was done on the grass outside our caravan.

A German came up to him, saying, "We have been watching you and your family! You all have been very polite and well mannered."

Now Michael was not in the mood to exchange pleasantries and grumpily replied, "Danke" (Thanks), still frantically looking for the car keys. He did eventually find them in one of the cases, among the clothes. They had

dropped out of the top pocket of his shirt when he was packing.

When all was stowed away, he felt a bit guilty about being so curt towards a well-meaning camper. So he found the German man out and said, "We have lots of army rations left over, which we brought on holiday with us. Rather than us taking them all the way back, would you like to use them up?" The man happily agreed, and so we handed over quite a lot of tinned and fresh food.

The next day, we were ready for the off—cases on the roof, children in the car, petrol in the tank, road map on my knees (satellite navigations systems were too pricey at that time)—and prepared for the long journey back. To our amazement, as we were driving off, all the German campers lined up and gave us a royal send-off, with waves and cries of, "Gute reise" (Safe travelling), ringing in our ears! We think they must have liked the army rations and told their friends. It was a lovely gesture.

Another Posting

The following day, we arrived back to our familiar surroundings in Kastanien Strasse, tired and bleary-eyed but looking back on the wonderful time we'd had as a family under a hot Italian sun. Sometime later, Mike came home with the information that we were to be posted to a Signal Regiment at a place called Krefeld. Once more we were in to the packing up routine and preparing the quarter, ready for another march out, with all the scrubbing, washing, polishing, ironing, dusting, and taking care of other details the accommodation service officer (ASA) looked for on inspections when moving out.

A week before we were due to move, all the ladies who worked at the teachers' accommodation quarters decided that I should have a farewell party. The day was set, and they presented me with a beautiful bouquet of flowers and a crystal cake stand. What I didn't know was they had spiked my Coca Cola and lemonade with gin, and they knew I did not drink alcohol. The rest of the morning was a blur, as I do

not recall anything except for sitting on the arm of a settee and then falling off it.

The rest of the story was told by Mike, when he called for me at lunchtime. He said, "I came to see how you were. I found you sitting on the floor giggling like a baby. Most of the ladies were not much better either. I picked you up and said, 'I think it's time you were at home.' Lots of loud cheery byes were called as I helped you to the door. It was raining hard, so you put the flowers that the ladies had given you over your head and carried your umbrella under your arm, while I carried the cake stand. When you got through our door, you went straight up the stairs on your hands and knees, and all I could see was a very 'shaky bottom' disappearing into our bedroom (still on hands and knees!). Within two minutes flat, you were asleep and snoring in a most unladylike manner.

"Later when I had to go back to work, I slipped up stairs to see how you were. By then, you were softly moaning, 'Oh my feet, my feet.' I said, 'Your feet! Don't you mean your head?' 'No,' you replied. 'My feet.'"

Since that day the location of my brains has always has been a joke in our house. The day came when we had to "stand by our beds"—an army expression for inspections. On the stroke of nine o'clock, our ASA turned up. He went through our quarter, and under the intensity of his glare, we stood and waited for him to look for the slightest flaw or mark on the army property. I think he was disappointed that he couldn't find anything he could charge us for.

We handed over the keys to our home where we had been for three years—we had said our goodbyes to all our friends and neighbours—and we were away. Our car was

packed to the roof with boxes, and there were packages all around our children, who were in the back somewhere. We set off to drive the 177 kilometres (110 miles) down to Krefeld. Despite the frequent cries of, "Are we there yet?" from the back seat and stops for the toilet, we eventually made it to our new address.

We weren't exactly in Krefeld but, rather, in a satellite area of army quarters just over 7 kilometres (4.5 miles) from the camp. Our new house turned out to be a flat on the first floor of a three-storey complex.

Now those who have experienced "flat life" will know a flat is totally different from a house, as it is communal living, where many rules and regulations apply (especially in Germany). No washing was to be hung outside on the balconies. The cleanliness of the common areas of each floor and stairs was the responsibility of the occupants living on that level. No cigarette ends or rubbish were to be thrown out of the windows. The stairs were to be swept and the banisters dusted. Every Sunday, everyone had to assemble outside the flat and walk round the block, picking up any litter that happened to be on the ground—which as mainly cigarette ends, sweets papers, and used fish and chip papers.

As Mike held the senior rank of the block, he had to make sure the rules were enforced. He was always in conflict with someone, as the people in the block made excuses for not doing a particular job. His main annoyance came from the people directly over our flat, as they would shake their carpets out on a Sunday afternoon over their balcony. All the dust would drift down through our windows just as we were sitting down to dinner, and all we would get were dust and gritty tastes in our mouths. Time and time again, he

would be up the stairs, banging on their door and telling them to "pack it in"!

Another gripe related to the requirement for each floor to keep its bit clean. The cleaners would simply sweep the dust and dirt over the edge of the stairs. Of course it would end up on the ground floor.

And to top it all, there were the soldiers and wives coming back from the bars at night. They would be shouting and giggling as they staggered up to their floor, so it was not a good introduction into communal living.

The Signals Regiment was given the title 28 Signal Regiment. It was part of the NATO forces, which, at that time, were working with the Belgians, the Dutch, and occasionally the Germans to boost and link up communications among the rest of the NATO allies. The regiment was away on exercises more than they were in camp.

Banking in St Tönis

Having moved from Osnabruck, it made sense to change our bank. Not too far from us was a Dresdner Bank, and so our accounts were transferred there. One day, Mike asked me to cash a cheque. So I drove the short distance to the bank and waited in the queue along with other customers. Then I heard from behind a glass panel a man saying, "Come."

Nobody moved. The direction was repeated, "Come."

Then I realised the man was looking at me. I nervously stepped out of the queue, not having done any German bank transactions before. I went forward, wondering if I was in the right queue. He smiled and took the cheque and gave it to the cashier, and I was given the cash. I felt very embarrassed, as people were still in the queue waiting to be served and staring at me with a who-does-she-think-she-is look. I quickly shot out of the bank and drove home.

A few weeks later, Michael asked me to cash another cheque. I reluctantly agreed. I drove up to the bank again

and, this time, waited in the car park, as it was not yet opening time. The next thing I knew was a loud bang on the roof of the car. It was that man again. "Come," he said. "You want money? I can see you from our camera inside, but you cannot see me. If you need money, you just knock on the door."

I said, "No. It is fine. I can wait."

"Nein," he said. "You come." He opened up a smaller door in the main massive front door and let me through.

Now I was very nervous, but there were other cashiers in the building. So I felt a little safer. Again he took my cheque and cashed it for me, letting me out just as a queue was starting to gather outside the door.

I made friends with a family on the top floor. The lady's name was Cindy. We even found jobs as cleaners in a men's hostel, while Aline and Anthony were at an English school some miles away.

Marie was now at kindergarten, and I managed to get her into the local German kindergarten. She was the first English child to get into the little school. She could speak no German. But after a few crying and screaming days of not wanting to go, she settled in and was very happy there. It was heart-wrenching to hear her sobbing and crying her little heart out, saying that she did not want to go. I desperately wanted to turn back and take her home. But I persevered, and soon she was letting go of my hand and running into the classroom. The German children were very curious about her, but she made friends and seemed to settle in.

One day, I had a call from the head of the kindergarten, asking if I could see her in her office. It turned out that Marie

was using some very bad words with the other children, which I did not understand, as she spoke no German. It turned out many of the others in her class were telling her all the swear words, which Marie was repeating in all innocence.

Sometime later, a much bigger boy pushed her into a rose bush, and she came out swearing and cursing at the boy who had done this.

After that, she never looked back and was soon conversing in fluent German. She was even talking to Mike in German and refusing to speak English. She would say, "Kein, Papa. Sie müssen Deutsch sprechen" (No, Daddy. You must speak German).

With the two older ones at school and Marie at the kindergarten, I, along with a lady from the top flat, managed to find a job working at a men's hostel. It was for English contractors who were not too far away working on heavy construction projects and run from an office of the PCLU (projects civilian liaison unit) in the camp. The hostel was very convenient to where the block of flats were. All we had to do was to clean the rooms and public areas, which was fairly simple work.

CHAPTER 31

A Flying Visitor
from Jamaica

While we were living at Uerdingen, I managed to persuade my uncle in Jamaica to come over for a holiday, and we paid for his airfare. Now the furthest Uncle had travelled was from Montego Bay to Kingston, a 110-mile trip by train, and he'd never been out of Jamaica. He was in his sixties, and we were concerned whether he would manage the journey. At that time, there was not a direct link from Jamaica into Germany. Rather, there was a flight that connected via Holland or France. To be on the safe side, Mike had to catch the ferry across to England to pick Uncle up from Heathrow and then travel back across Holland into Germany and then up to Krefeld and finally to our flat in Uerdingen.

Oh, it was such a joy to see him again after fourteen years of absence; he was the man who had brought me up from a very small child to when I got married. He was the man who had cooked, washed, and ironed for me until I was

old enough to manage for myself. He was the man who had stood by me when my real father wanted to take me away to another woman and then leave me again. He was the man who had wholeheartedly supported me in my marriage to Michael. I was so happy.

He was a big hit with our children and all the people in the block and was soon known to everyone as 'Uncle". Sometimes when I got back from work, he would be nowhere to been seen, only to find out he had been invited by the lady upstairs to make 'johnnycakes' (a bit like dumplings, only fried) for them and their family. Or he would be found by the railway lines down the street from where we lived. He had been a railway man all his life and just loved to see the big German trains go thundering past.

Another time when he couldn't be found at either of his favourite haunts, he was down by the river (the Rhine) and talking to a lady.

I said, "But, Uncle, you cannot speak any German."

"Never mind that," he said. "We got on real good and spent a pleasant afternoon talking about everything."

He was invited to the WOs & Sgts' Mess (warrant officers and sergeants' mess), where he made friends with everyone he met and was soon known as Uncle.

His time with us seemed over all too quick. The final touch was when I came into his bedroom one morning with a cup of tea, and he was sitting up in bed with his hat on and the blankets huddled around his shoulders. "Uncle," I said, "why do you have your hat on in bed?"

"Miss May," he replied. "I am *cold*, so *cold*." It was mid-October, and the heating in the block did not go on until the end of the month; the building was cooling down after

a lovely summer. I think it was with a mixture of sadness and gladness that his stay with us had come to an end. He was sad to go and leave our family and newfound friends but so glad to get back to the warmth and heat of Jamaica.

We found out there was now a direct flight from Dusseldorf to Jamaica, and there was no need for Uncle to catch the ferry back to the United Kingdom. The day arrived, and many in the block came to see Uncle off.

The place seemed quiet without him. Not long after Uncle had gone back home, Mike put a case forward to the CO (commanding officer) for the young soldiers living in the barracks to have extra sports activities in the evening. Most of them spent their time either in the bars in the town or just lying on their beds in camp. Mike was prepared to run basketball, indoor football, keep-fit classes, badminton, indoor hockey, and circuit training for them and anyone else who wanted to use the gym in the evening.

This idea was approved, and all we had to do was wait until a quarter became available where the "key personnel" were housed. This was just around the corner from the camp itself, a small cul-de-sac of English-occupied houses. Now, key personnel were the men who were important in setting the plans into action in case of an attack by foreign forces. This was still in the seventies when the United Kingdom was on high alert over Russia and the Cold War.

And thinking about the cold. The winter came and, with it, the snow and ice. One snowy morning. I was taking our youngest to the kindergarten. I was in my little NSU, an offshoot of the Audi/Volkswagen car that I'd received as a Christmas present from Mike. When I was approaching the traffic lights, suddenly the wheels slid away from me, and I

was spinning round and round and heading straight for a shop window. At the last moment, my wheels gripped, and I managed to straighten up.

"Oooooh, Mummy," cried Rachel. "That was lovely. Do it again." Oh the innocence of small children!

CHAPTER 32

Another Army Quarter
to Take Over

Months went by when news came that we were to be given a quarter very near the camp, which was where the key personnel lived. Great! No more communal flat living. No more Mike having to argue with people who were supposed to clean up their areas. No more carpet dust floating down from the flat above. No more Saturday parades of litter cleaning. I was sorry to leave my little job in the men's hostel but so glad to get away from all the aggravation of living where we were.

The ladies had a little farewell party for me but nothing like the one I'd experienced at the teachers' mess in Osnabruck. Even the manager, who was a rather dour man, gave me a large box of Black Magic chocolates, referring to my colour and a thank you for the cleaning I had done.

Once again, we were in march-out mode, and all the usual chores were done and checked off. Aline and Anthony were excited for the new move, and Marie would have to

leave her little kindergarten school and friends. But that was army life. As the major with those bright blue piercing eyes had said all those years ago when I was being interviewed to marry Michael, "Being an army wife is not easy, and you will be following him to wherever he is posted"

And so one spring morning, we were "marched in" to our new quarter, again with all the usual military thoroughness of inspecting and checking everything in the house.

Some weeks later, Mike said, "I saw a lovely tropical poster in the bank and asked the manager if, when they had finished with it, it would be possible for me have it. The manager said he would bring it." It was a Saturday when I was in the kitchen and looked up to see a man on a bicycle with a parcel under his arm. Oh no! It was that man from the bank. I wondered how he knew where we lived, but as Mike pointed out, he would have our address from our records held at the bank. I quickly slipped upstairs while he greeted him and invited him in. I didn't know it at the time; the man was the bank manager of the Dresdner bank.

I felt I was being rude by hiding upstairs so came down and made us all a cup of tea. He turned out to be a very nice person, who had come with the poster he had promised Mike weeks ago. We still have it now—a picture of a young couple holding hands while walking along a palm-fringed beach and the blue Caribbean Sea lapping at the edges of white sands. We got on so well we invited him and his wife for tea the following week. And the friendship has grown from there; we still value it to this day. We have spent holidays at their place, and they have had holidays at ours.

CHAPTER 33

Jubilee Celebrations

In 1977, June of that year, the queen celebrated her silver jubilee anniversary. It was celebrated with large-scale parties and parades throughout England and Commonwealth countries. We, in Germany had our own street party, as many British bases did across the world. Our cul-de-sac was transformed into a blaze of red, white, and blue flags, bunting, doors, curtains, and street lamps. All the children dressed in the colours of our national flag. Doorsteps, flowers, lamp posts, and anything else that could be decorated was decorated. We had tables laid out the length of the street, all covered in red, white, and blue paper cloths and mountains of food supplied by the cookhouse. All who gathered had to bring their own drinks. This came in rivers of beers wines and spirits. We invited the local German neighbours, as it was a party that was to go right on throughout the night, and it did! But what a success it was, and there were many bleary-eyed hangover headaches the next morning on parade to clear up the revelries of the night before.

Later on in the year, Jubilee Medals were awarded to certain people in the regiment. Michael was very honoured to receive one, as only eight per regiment or corps was issued, and the commanding officer could have easily given it to another of his own men.

Thinking back to commanding officers, sometime after we were posted to 28 Signal Regiment, I went to the PCLU (personnel and civilian liaison unit), which found work for wives and young adults, to see if there were any jobs to be had. There was a vacancy for a housekeeper at the commanding officer's house. Would I be interested? I said I would like to try and see if I liked it. I was given the address where he lived and was asked to report on Monday morning at 0900 hours.

This I duly did, only to find that Mrs Byrne, the CO's wife, was unsure if she was allowing anyone else to be the housekeeper, as she had been let down so many times by the previous one. She would let me know!

A week later, I was asked to see Mrs Byrne at her quarters. There she ran through the list of duties I would be required to do. It was mainly looking after the house and keeping it clean and tidy. I was to cook when necessary, mainly for her children when they came from school and other small jobs that occasionally turned up.

I soon settled into a routine, and by lunchtime, I was normally finished. Her children were twins, Kaitlin and Kayla, and the eldest, Tanya. She loved to be around me, and we spent many happy hours in the kitchen singing or dancing. And best of all, they loved my cooking. Mrs Byrne was a pleasant person to get on with and soon put me at ease.

I was there for about a year when the order came

through that the CO was to be posted, this time to Abu Dhabi in the United Arab Emirates. So there was lots of packing and preparation for the move. This meant my time as housekeeper was coming to an end. When the new commanding officer, Lt Col Eames, and his wife, Anne, arrived to take over the quarter, they asked if I would like to continue as before.

I accepted, and life and the routine carried on in much the same way. The new CO and his wife had two children, Brenda and Robin. They were much older than the Byrnes children but equally polite and accepted me as part of the household, and we all got on extremely well. That was especially the case with Anne.

CHAPTER 34

Jamaican Sunshine

The months rolled by, and Christmas came round again. I remember Christmas Day as if it was yesterday. The children were running around all excited. Father Christmas had been and gone (Mike heavily disguised as Santa himself!), which left us to open our own presents. One of mine seemed very heavy. I jokingly said, "What's this? A brick?" It turned out it *was* a brick.

I looked at it wondering what I was to do with it, and then Mike said, "Turn it over." On the underside was a ticket. It was a ticket for a three-week holiday to Jamaica. I was so overcome, I burst into tears.

When I regained my self-control, I was wondering about my job, the children, the house, and all sorts of questions that were racing through my mind. He laughingly replied, "Don't worry. It's all taken care of."

It turned out it was the best kept secret kept by all the neighbours in the street and all the children, both young

and old, who knew at least six weeks before about my trip to Jamaica.

The day came when my bag was packed, and I was ready to fly. I was to stay at the Salvation Army School for the Blind and Visually Handicapped. Major Gladys Lucario was in charge of the school and this had all been arranged by Mike. Oh! What a welcome I received when entering the school gates. Many of the young girls who I had looked after were still at the school. There were lots of hugs and kisses and squeals of delight, and the girls felt my face and hair to see how much I had changed. They had certainly grown.

It was lovely to feel the hot Jamaican sunshine on my skin again and see the tall tropical palm trees with their fronds waving in the breeze or to catch a bus to downtown Kingston and to see the bustle of the markets and the colour of the many fruits. The time passed very quickly.

CHAPTER 35

Back to Germany Again

Soon it was time to take the plane back to Germany. After tearful farewells from the children at the school, I left the warmth of a tropical island and made the long flight back to the much cooler climate of Dusseldorf Airport in Germany. Mike was there grinning like a Cheshire cat, overjoyed to see me again. I had so many questions to ask. How were the children? Did they get enough to eat? Did they get to school on time? Did they get cooked meals? How did the lady who stood in for me at the Eames get on? Did you manage to get the washing done? And all sorts of other questions.

Mike assured me that everything was fine, and we still had three clean fine very healthy children who were longing to meet their mum. And Mrs Eames was looking forward to seeing me again. It was back to normal routine, with the memories of my holiday fading fast. Sometime later, I was invited to join the wives club run by the colonel's wife and spent mornings with like-minded wives who experienced the same joys and tears of bringing up a family while their

husbands were away on manoeuvres with other NATO countries.

With the club, there was a trip to Berlin, and I was asked if I would like to go. At first I wasn't sure, but under Mike's encouragement I agreed. The day came when a party of us set off on a train from Krefeld to travel the 381 kilometres (237 miles) to Berlin. The trip was uneventful until we reached the Russian border, when officials came and thoroughly checked our passports. All the laughter and chattering died away, as these stern unsmiling men looked carefully at each photo before passing on to the next person. We moved off again, while having an afternoon cup of tea in our carriage.

There came several loud *crack*s at the windows. It turned out that someone had been taking shots at the train, which carried the Union Jack flag on the side of the carriages. Luckily, no one was hurt, and the windows were only chipped. But it sent the guards into a bit of a flap and a helicopter was ordered to escort the train all the way to Berlin.

On our arrival at the hotel we were staying in, we were paired off, two to a room. I could see the look on the girl's face when she was told I was her room partner. I pretended not to notice as we went to the room we had been allotted. She was not from 28 Signal Regiment but 16 Signal Regiment, who were actually based in the town of Krefeld and not on the outskirts as we were. I chattered away quite normally, and I could see her relaxing. For the rest of our stay we became firm friends.

We had trips to well-known parts of the city. We visited the Berlin Stadium, where Hitler held the famous 1936 Olympic Games. Even now after all those years there was

still an atmosphere of suspense and excitement. We saw the Berlin Wall and Checkpoint Charlie, which was the barrier or crossing point between East and West Berlin. We visited the Berlin radio tower (Funkturm) locally known as "the long beanpole" and had marvellous views of the city from its 150-metre (450-foot) vantage point. We visited Spandau Prison and actually saw Rudolf Hess walking around in the yard. He was Hitler's right-hand man before he flew to Britain and was captured. Spandau Prison was demolished in 1987 after his death, to prevent it from becoming a neo-Nazi shrine. And we were given what every wife loved—free shopping time, on the long broad Kurfürstendamm, one of the most famous streets in Berlin.

On our last day, my newfound friend and I decided to have breakfast in bed and ordered it over the telephone from our hotel room. Very soon, a very young handsome waiter came and served us our breakfast. Giggling like schoolgirls, we thoroughly enjoyed our meal.

We made ourselves ready and went down to meet the other wives waiting in the lobby—to be greeted with, "Where have you been? You have missed breakfast."

When we told the others what we had done, they were amazed. The hotel staff also told us that we did not have to pay the room service charge, and that was the best breakfast I ever tasted!

Soon we were back on the train to Krefeld with no further mishaps. Our time with 28 Signal Regiment was coming to an end—not anther posting but the end career of Michael's twenty-five years in the army (or twenty-seven and a half if you include his boy soldier service). We had been back to England a number of times when on leave and

had been house hunting. Some of the properties we viewed were awful, some lovely but sadly out of our price range. We eventually settled on a house on the edge of Telford at Hadley in Shropshire. Some years before, when we were at Park Hall Camp, we had always said we would like to settle in the county, as the people were so warm and friendly.

We had lots of farewell parties with friends and officers who were very sorry to see us go, and the crowning moment was at the last regimental mess dinner when Mike was hoisted on to the shoulders of his comrades and carried around the room to cheers and well wishes on our coming back to England.

CHAPTER 36

Return to England

All our belongings were packed and on a rainy day in 1978. The removal van arrived to take our belongings back to the United Kingdom. We were to follow by car after our last march out. We were told by the ASA that we were not to bother too much about cleaning the quarter, as electricians were moving in to rewire the place as soon as we had moved out. We could not do it; after all the years of cleaning, scrubbing, polishing, and washing, we left the quarter in the normal spotless condition and our consciences were clear.

Once more, the car was packed to capacity. Inside with me, Mike, Aline, Anthony, and Marie was as much as we could possibly pile around us, mainly breakables. In fact, we were acting as packaging.

We took the long drive across Germany through Belgium to arrive at Zeebrugge for the Ferry to Dover. The trip was uneventful, and the long journey up to Shropshire was broken by toilet stops or brief rests from driving.

We finally arrived in Hadley at our new home. There

was no sign of our furniture or belongings, which had been packed off a week before. We found out that the furniture van had delivered all we owned a few days before and left everything on the driveway in the pouring rain. Our next-door neighbour had taken his car out of his garage and pushed our possessions into his car space, leaving his car on the drive until we arrived. This was very nice of the neighbours, and we were very grateful.

We now had to settle down to a new life and a new way of becoming civilians. No more Mike away on sports meetings or manoeuvres with the army. No more dinner nights and a chance to dress up. No more wives club and the club's activities. No more march ins or outs of army quarters and many other things we had to adapt to.

When we had settled in to our new home, I realised a long time before we left Germany that the place was too small for our now growing teenage family. It had looked fine when the place was empty. But now furnished, it was cramped and hard to move around. We had to find a larger house.

CHAPTER 37

House Hunting

The first priority was to find schools for our children. We found suitable places for them. Luckily, Mike was on leave until September, when he was finally discharged from the army. That made it easier for us to sort out the many questions that cropped up while getting used to civilian life. We had to register with a medical and a dental centre; arrange house insurance; get road tax for driving in England; and transfer our savings into an English bank, as we were no longer registered with the Dresdner Bank in Germany. And there were many other details that we had to know about. Transition from being a soldier or a soldier's wife to civilian life was not an easy one.

The next big problem was for Michael to find work. There was not much call for physical training instructors, and most of the local schools had their own. An interview became available to become an ASA for the MOD (Ministry of Defence), and as Mike was well versed in marching in

and out of army quarters, he applied, along with five other applicants.

He must have said the right things because he was accepted. He was asked to start work as soon as possible. This was at Donnington, and he would be required to look after the married quarters, the barracks, and the units that were based there. That was ideal for him as the depot was only three miles (four and a half kilometres) from where we lived.

Now the next big problem was our house. Our children were falling over themselves in the rooms they had, and a great deal of our furniture was still stored in our garage. Finding a larger home to live in became a priority. Once again, we were house-hunting—scouring the newspapers, calling at estate agents, and arranging appointments with house sellers. All the houses we visited and liked came with it, big prices.

We eventually settled on one that seemed to suit our purposes. We were just going through the door to visit the house owners when the phone rang. It was from a friend who had just seen a for sale notice in a window of a big house along the Trench Road. Might it be worth a look? So along the Trench Road we went and eventually came to the house in question. We knocked on the door, apologised we had not made an appointment, and explained we'd been told about the place by a friend who had seen the house was for sale.

The lady invited us in, and as soon as I stepped inside the door, I said to Michael, "Oh, yes. I feel so at home. This is just right. Let's buy this one."

To this, he replied, "Hang on. We don't even know the price."

I just knew we had found the proper place. It was so friendly and comfortable; it was if the house was saying to me, "Welcome home, May."

"Oh, Mike, we must find a way to have this one. Pleeease."

And so it was in mid-December we moved into our new home. And so began our adjusting and settling down to civilian life—in our new house and together at last. It seems such a long time ago, and memories fade, leaving you thinking, *Did that really happen?*

Some incidents really do stand out. One such incident involved the heating in the home. There were three industrial-sized storage heaters, each about as big as a large coffee table. There was one in the bedroom, one in the hall, and one in the dining room. They took up a great deal of space. The best heater to keep us warm was in our bedroom. The children would bring their clothes from their bedrooms to ours to get dressed. The house was cold and, being December, the heaters were working full blast and producing very little heat. Again I thought, *What have I let myself into, on leaving my warm tropical country?* Those heaters were very expensive to run, and in our first four weeks in the house, we had a large bill of £60 (in today's 2017 prices, around £270.6p).

We decided to get a different source of heat and settled for central heating throughout. This was done in the New Year, as we had Christmas to get through. We had lots of quotes and estimates and eventually settled on one that seemed reasonable and would meet our needs.

Early in January, the contractor turned up and started to drill for radiator fittings. Dust and noise was everywhere, and the contractor remarked, "You have a very strong house

here. I have already gone through two masonry drills, and I think I'll have to buy another one." We found out later that the original builder had built the house for himself using only the top-quality materials.

The three massive heaters were dismantled and sleek slimline radiators were fitted in every room except the kitchen. When it was completed, Oh! We had the joy of feeling warm and comfortable again.

It then became apparent that we were leaking too much heat through the walls, so cavity wall filling had to be paid for. Around that, time the government had introduced financial help with loft insulation, which we applied for and got the grant.

Our next project was double glazing, for which we got several quotes. And in spring of that year, the windows were replaced. So, as the old saying goes, "We were as snug as a bug in a rug" in our own home.

We thought it was about time we gave ourselves a holiday and we settled for Tenerife in the Canary Islands at Puerto de la Cruz, on the north side of the island. For those who have been there, you will remember that side of the island is very green.

CHAPTER 38

Holiday Time

We were all looking forward to going up to the top of an extinct volcano Mount Teide the highest point on the island. But when we got near the top, the cable car, which takes you to the peak, could not run because it was too windy. So instead the coach took us down into the crater where they filmed *One Million Years B.C.* (That's where Raquel Welch made her rise to stardom.) There were all sorts of strange rock formations, which had been thrown up by volcanic eruptions. That was where parts of *The Ten Commandments* were filmed (like when Charlton Heston as Moses brought down the Ten Commandments from Mount Sinai).

Looking back, I recall that we've visited Tenerife four times. During three of those trips, we tried to get to the top of the mountain and never made it. On the first, it was too windy. The second time, there was too much snow on top. The third, the company operating the cable car was on strike. The fourth and last time was a flying four-day visit

to the resort of Adeje, and we didn't even bother to attempt the peak.

On the third run to Mount Teide, when we arrived by coach at the place where you transfer to the cable car, it was not running. The guide requested, "Please do not pick up any of the lava that is around."

Well I only wanted just a little piece, so I found a small lump and popped it in to my bag. I must confess I did feel a bit guilty.

In to the coach we went and started off. We'd only travelled about 400 metres off the flank of the mountain when a policeman stepped out in front of the coach and flagged it down. Oh no! Had they seen me put the lump of lava in to my bag? What could I do? Where could I put this seemingly now enormous lump of rock? I really didn't want to spend time in a Spanish prison! Oh! I wished I hadn't picked it up. What was I to do?

I quickly got it out and rolled the offending chunk under the seats of the coach. I could hear it going *clunk, clunk, clunk* as it rolled farther down the bus. I sat looking all demure and innocent in my seat, but my heart was pounding inside.

The policeman did not come into the coach but was talking to the driver. It turned out that there was a car accident a bit farther down the mountain, and the driver had to be careful when getting around the wreckage.

Down the winding twisty roads we went until we got to our resort. Luckily, we were the last ones to be dropped off, and so out we went, all bent and stooped as we made our

way down the bus looking under the seats for my piece of lava. I still have it now, and every so often, Mike will bring it down and with great joy tell our guests the story of the lump of lava.

Testing Time in Wellington

A few months after we had settled into our house, I asked a policeman how long I could drive on my international driving license, which I'd had when in Germany. He wasn't sure but thought it was about a year. So I decided to apply for an English one to be on the right side of the law.

I applied, and found out that I had to take the English driving test. A few weeks later, a letter came asking me to attend the test centre in Wellington for a nine o'clock appointment. I was not too nervous, as I had been driving in Germany for about five and a half years.

The instructor was unsmiling and very formal, saying, "Turn left here, madam." "Turn right at the next roundabout, madam." "I want you to reverse in to here, madam."

All this I was doing quite easily. I was on a straight piece of road when, a woman with a pram walked past a pedestrian crossing and then suddenly turned back onto it, causing me to jam on my brakes hard.

We continued the test, but when we got back to the

starting point, he said, "Madam, you have failed, as you should have anticipated the lady's actions at the pedestrian crossing."

I was furious. When I got home, I said to Mike, "That's it! I am not going to take another test, especially with such a miserable-looking man."

Mike was sympathetic but advised me to resit the test, as a driving license would give me my independence and would be useful if he couldn't drive at some time. After I had cooled down, I could see the sense and reapplied. Months later, I had a letter asking me to attend the test centre at the same place as before.

The day came, and I was waiting in the office for the test examiner when, to my horror, the same miserable-looking man came into the room and called out my name. Oh No! Not him again? With a sinking heart, I followed him out to the car.

Off we went. He was stern, unsmiling, and exactly the same as he had been on our previous encounter—madam this and madam that. We took the same route, with the same pedestrian crossing and the same reversing area. At last it was over. Still unsmiling, he said, "Madam, you have passed." Oh! Thank goodness. Now I could get on with my life.

CHAPTER 40

My Life as an Auxiliary Nurse

I started looking for a job and used to look in the local papers. A lady, who I knew, suggested that I should try at the Royal Hospital in Wolverhampton. I applied and had an interview with the senior nursing officer. A few days later, a letter arrived asking if I could start the coming Friday night as an auxiliary nurse.

The time came, and I drove to Wolverhampton, arriving a little nervous and wondering what to expect. I was put on Sheldon and Langley wards (named after prominent physicians) and quickly shown what to do and what was expected of me. The duties were many and varied in those days.

I went on an auxiliary nurse's course. You learnt a lot on the job directed by nurses and matrons. I changed many sheets, gave out numerous bedpans, assisted patients with their feeding, and helped to get them in and out of beds. I also helped lay out bodies from the morgue.

I remember one old lady who was severely injured in a car crash and not expected to live. The doctors had prescribed TLC (tender loving care) only and to just keep her comfortable.

When I came on duty I used to see how she was progressing and told her that I prayed for her recovery. One night I saw her struggling to drink but unable to manage the tumbler. I suggested she hold the glass in both hands and perhaps that would help? She was very grateful and found it was a way of drinking and feeding herself. I know as a nurse you had to be professional, but I must admit, I had a special feeling for this elderly lady. A week later when back on duty, I looked for her and found that the bed was empty. My first thought was that she had died.

Later when we all sat down and listened to the reports on each patient, I realised she had made a tremendous recovery and had been sent home for assessment to see if she could manage in her own home.

We never saw her again, so she had passed all the tests and was up and about once more. It made us feel so good.

One Christmas Eve, we did our shift, which was a fairly quiet one; many of the patients had been sent home, which was the normal practice then for Christmas. And for once the hours seemed to drag slowly by. Come the morning, we clocked off, and I was eager to get back to the family for Christmas Day.

The roads were quiet, and I sped through deserted villages and countryside, eager to get back and see the children open their presents. I pulled in to the drive; I unlocked the front door, expecting to hear excited cries from our family, only to be met by a dead silence—not a sound.

They were all fast asleep, wrapped up like mummies. I was quite annoyed, having done a full night shift and then to rush home to a non-existent Christmas morning.

Not long after that, back at work, a team of us were struggling to lift a very heavy lady back into her bed. As we heaved her on to the bed, my shoulder gave way, and she landed full weight on my arm, trapping it underneath her. The pain that shot through my shoulder was agonising. I thought I was going to pass out. I disentangled myself from the lady and went back on to the ward, rubbing my arm and shoulder. Little did I realise that one action was to take over my life. For the rest of my time, I've had constant pain and operations on my shoulder, which I still live with today.

Another occasion that further damaged my shoulder happened when I was driving home after a busy night shift. I saw some cars that had skidded over the road and realised the roads were like glass due to the ice that had built up overnight. I too hit the ice and felt myself skidding sideways towards a ditch and a hedge. The car gave a jolt as it hit the verge, flipped onto its side and ended up in a deep ditch. The safety belt saved me from serious injury, but I had landed on my already painful and sore shoulder. I couldn't get out of the driver's door due to the car resting on that side. I clambered over to the back seat and got out that way. I looked up to see a group of men just staring at me. I shouted up to them, "I am all right."

Startled, they clambered down the bank and helped me up to the top of the road. I said, "I have to get down again, as I have left some money in the car, which I was going to use for the family shopping." Two men said, "You stay here. We will go and look."

They came back, saying, "Sorry. There is no money there." I said, "Yes, it is definitely there. Let me go and check."

They said, "No. It's all right. We will go and have another look." They scrambled down the bank, looked inside the car again, and shouted up, "Yes it's okay. We've found it." I was still in shock, but there was something not quite right about their actions, and I think they had found the money and were going to keep it! If true, how could they take advantage of such a life-frightening situation?

Another kind gentleman drove me to the medical centre, where I was checked over. The doctor said," Go to bed and rest." I phoned Mike and told him of the situation and then went to bed, as my shoulder was extremely painful.

I had to phone in to work and say I would not be at the hospital for my shift, as I was in too much pain. Not long after that incident, I had to stop work; I could not carry on doing the duties expected of me. Later, I was informed by the senior nursing officer and senior administrator who came to visit me that, as I had not put my first mishap with the heavy patient in the accident book, I would not be entitled to any compensation.

To be honest, I never gave it a thought. To me, my compensation was helping seriously ill patients get better and go home.

I had two operations on my shoulder over the years, but neither was successful, and I have suffered constant pain since.

When I was feeling a little better, Mike started looking for a holiday just to get away for a while. I think having travelled around and moved so many times while we were

still in the army, we still had the urge to go and see different places. So as a family, we all took a trip to Majorca and stayed at Can Picafort. It was then a small holiday resort on the north-western part of the island.

What sticks in my mind was the long cycle ride around the bay to Alcúdia, another resort some sixteen miles round trip back to Can Picafort. Oh! My bottom was sore for days afterwards. We were very impressed with the Caves of Drach (Dragons Caves) and were expecting to go into the side of a mountain.

But no. It was into a field and then to an open hole in the ground leading down to the caves (probably changed by now). The rock formations were fascinating and all lit up. At the very bottom of the cave was a large natural amphitheatre with a lake of completely still, clear water. We were all seated around the lake, and a boatman with a small ensemble of musicians came slowly across the water playing "Tales of Hoffmann". It was a magical experience, and the acoustics were remarkable.

Talking about acoustics, both Mike and I played in the Salvation Army band, and there was an advert in *The War Cry* (the Salvation Army newspaper). Musicians were wanted to play in France at Christmastime. The airfare, accommodation, and feeding arrangements would all be paid for by the local Salvation Army corps. Michael applied and was accepted with many others to be sent out to different towns around the country. He and three others were to play in the small town near Montpellier in Southern France.

In mid-December, he left for Heathrow Airport (on my birthday!) along with the three other bandsmen. There was Alf from Liverpool and, from Leicester, Brian and Gerald.

Alf was the prime mover and organiser of the little quartet, as he could speak very good French.

They all played there for several years with the French Salvation Army or Armée du Salut as it is known France and always left on my birthday. It was a standing joke about the lengths Mike went to so as not to give me birthdays present.

They thought they we're going to play in French southern sunshine, but it was not to be, for the town was in a valley where cold winds from the mountains all funnelled down to that little township. They were kept very busy playing carols around the town starting at nine in the morning until one o'clock. They then went back to the quarters for lunch and were back out at two o'clock until six in the evening. It was a heavy and demanding schedule, especially with only four playing. They used to come back to England totally drained and usually on Christmas Eve.

CHAPTER 41

The Crash

One day, Aline, our eldest daughter, came to us asking if she could go to an evening fashion show with some friends she had met at a disco (a word hardly ever used these days; *clubbing* is the in word, as it sounds more grown-up and racy). Aline has always been a sensible and level-headed girl, so we gave our consent.

The evening came, and off she went with three others in a car to the show. Time passed, more time passed, and nothing was heard from Aline. We were getting restless and worried. It was now half past three in the morning, and she had never been this late before. Green and I couldn't sleep and kept going to the window in the hope of seeing the car pull into the drive

In the end, he said, "I am going to call the police." I had this dreadful premonition that something horrific had happened to her. As he made his way towards the telephone, it rang. It was the police, asking if Mr Michael was the

father of a girl called Aline who had been involved in a fatal accident.

My blood ran cold. Oh no! Not our precious daughter? The police said the car carrying the four young people had hit a lamp post killing, one and severely injuring the others. They were in a Midland Accident and Emergency Department. The driver was killed. Aline suffered extensive bruising and cuts on her arms and legs and a compound fracture of the nose and had an eyelid nearly torn off. Apparently, the driver fell asleep at the wheel and crashed into a lamp post.

We rushed down the motorway to the hospital, found the A & E department, and were directed to the room where she was. The surgeon had just finished sewing her eyelid back on, and she was still coming around from the anaesthesia. There was glass all over the floor, which we had to walk through. He'd been picking broken shards out from her arms, legs, eyelid, and nose.

The surgeon said that Aline was the luckiest of the four. The driver was dead on impact. The other girl had her spine shattered and would have to wear a steel corset for life, and the girl's friend had suffered brain damage.

A few days later, when we had got her home, she was still too badly injured to wash and dress herself. I had to do all this despite the pain she was in. Now, Aline was a beautiful girl who turned so many heads. The thought of the damaged eyelid and a scarring across the bridge of her nose, arms, and legs really turned her into a recluse who was afraid to go out or even speak to anyone outside the family.

It was during this time that she was offered a job in an optician's shop in the town. But of course she could not go,

as she was still recovering. The owner of the business said she was prepared to wait until she was completely healed, which was very nice of the lady.

In the end after many arguments about how she was acting, we managed to persuade her to see her solicitor who said, "If I give you some foolscap paper, will you write down everything you remember and how you are feeling."

Aline eventually gave him back three sheets of A4 paper, closely written on both sides telling how she'd felt during her accident. The solicitor realised she was suffering from psychological as well as physical damage and treated her case for both incidents.

Having listened to the solicitor and releasing all her pent-up feelings on paper, she slowly came back to her normal shy but pleasant self.

CHAPTER 42

Wedding Fever

Two important events come to mind related to when our son announced that he was moving out into a flat. He was finding his independence, and it seemed strange not to have him come home after a day's work. Being a mother, I still worried about him and used to take meals up to his flat, which was not too far away.

Several months later, he announced he was going to marry his girlfriend, Lindsey. This came as a surprise to us, as he'd never expressed a wish to get settled. So there were plans and preparations to be made.

Usually the mother and father of the bride arrange the wedding arrangements. But Lindsey's father had put his foot down and said, "No more expenses, as you and your sisters have relied on me for far too long. Now it is your turn to pay your way." So she and Anthony came to us for advice and help. They sorted out the wedding ceremony and the reception at a Methodist Church, while we went ahead with the arrangements for the night party and discotheque.

Come the day of the wedding, our son looked so young yet so smart in his top hat and tails. The day was bright but breezy, and everyone seemed relaxed and happy. Lots of pictures were taken for the special day, and the reception was held in a hotel in the town of their choosing.

That year, it was our twenty-fifth wedding anniversary and our son's twenty-first birthday. So we held a double celebration. Twenty-five years—where had the time gone? And looking back, I recall happy times of love, laughter, and the sharing of many experiences and family times together.

We wanted to celebrate this milestone in our lives and put out invitations to our many friends to attend a celebration dinner and party at the Charlton Hotel (sadly no longer used as a hotel). Anthony's friends and ours came from far and wide, bringing presents for him and silver presents for us, as twenty-five years is a tradition for anything silver to be given. We had so many silver presents that we had to buy another glass cabinet so everything could be displayed.

Aline bought us a holiday in Majorca for a week, staying in a hotel in Magaluf. After all those years, the hotel is still there, now run by a different company. And Magaluf did not hold the same reputation as it does today, as a mecca for young people and all the high jinks they get up to in the resort. Looking back, it was a wonderful year.

Wedding plans seemed to be in the air, for Aline, now fully recovered from her injuries, was asked by her fiancé, Frank, if he could marry her. It was all done very formally, as he came to our house looking very smart in a suit and asking if he could have our daughter's hand in marriage. We were delighted. Frank was a very steady level-headed boy.

So the planning and preparations went ahead. Our

daughter would talk over the many details with me in the early hours of the morning, as she could not sleep, and we spent many shopping trips to Birmingham looking for the right dress or gown for that one-time special occasion. In the end, she ordered the dress from Italy.

The wedding was to be held in September. It was another top hat and tails affair. And there were the usual last-minute panic and alarms, as the bouquets were late in coming and hairdressing took longer than expected.

Aline looked like a fairy-tale princess when she walked down the aisle with a very proud dad holding her arm. Wedding vows were exchanged, and the ceremony was over.

The reception was held at a place called the Buck Hotel. It is believed to have derived its name from stag hunting days, when a buck was found there in the fork of a tree. The hotel is nestled near the bottom of the Wrekin, a local beauty spot and prominent hill that dominates the landscape for many miles around. Another wonderful and successful wedding celebration went off for a young couple in our family as they started off in life as Mr and Mrs Morrisey.

With the wedding over, my body relaxed, and I was feeling very tired. All the early morning talks with Aline had caught up with me, and I just wanted to sleep. Mike thought it would be a good idea if we got away for a weekend break and to unwind from the stresses and emotional strains of wedding planning. We thought a trip up to the Lake District National Park in Cumbria sounded relaxing enough, and so we found and rang a bed and breakfast house in the area.

We left on a Friday morning and travelled the 186 miles (299 kilometres) up to the Lake District. I didn't know much about it, as I slept all the way there, only to wake up

when Michael was shaking my shoulder, saying, "Wake up, dear. We have arrived."

We booked into our room, and the bed looked so inviting I just threw myself on it. The next thing I knew, he was gently shaking me again, saying, "Come on, sleepyhead. We had better get something to eat for our tea."

I had slept right through until the light was fading. Michael had been out exploring the town. We walked around the town, which wasn't very big and had a meal in a cafe somewhere. Mike said there was a lecture on at Moot Hall, which was the local information centre. For those who do not know it, the current building was erected in 1813 and, since then, has served as a courthouse, a prison, a museum, a town hall, and even a butter and fruit market! Anyway, that evening they were talking about how the lakes were formed during the last glacial ice age. I could hardly keep my eyes open and was very glad when it was over. Mike found it interesting.

So we went back to the house where we were staying and a quick wash and cleaning my teeth and then into my pyjamas and onto the bed and, well, then it was morning. What had happened to the night?

The sun was shining through the curtains, and it was looking to be a good day. Breakfast was a huge plate of everything you could think of, and the owner had great pleasure in telling me that he had been to Jamaica. Loved the food, loved the rum, and loved the reggae. I did promise him when we came again I would bring him some jerk chicken. Poor man is still waiting, as we haven't up that way for years.

We decided to take a drive around the nearest lake to

the town. Soon we saw a glint of water through the trees, and the road followed it down to the lake itself. It all looked very peaceful, and the water was quite still, giving off a lovely reflection of the mountains on the other side. About halfway round, Mike pulled on to a grassy bank on the side of the road to take in the view. We got out of the car and sat on a large flat piece of rock about the size of a large table.

We sat for a while, and then Mike said, "You wait here while I go exploring up in the hills." I readily agreed, for climbing hills is not one of my favourite pastimes.

He set off and was soon a distant figure going up this mountain. The sun was warm on my face, so I decided to lie back on the rock. I could see small white fluffy clouds drifting by and birds wheeling and turning overhead. I heard the rippling of a stream emptying somewhere into the lake. The trees by the lake were making rustling and whispering noises. It all seemed so peaceful and quiet. I could feel myself relaxing.

The next thing I knew, Mike was back, saying, "Hey sleepy bones, you have been here for hours. I got to the top of the mountain and could see you way down below, stretched out on the rock flat on your back like you were waiting to be sacrificed. It's time to go back for late lunch or tea."

I had slept and slept nearly the whole time we were at the lakes and in the guest house and right through the weekend. I'd never been a good sleeper and seemed to have used all my sleep up on that one weekend.

Sleep has been always a long time coming, as my mind is constantly turning over or thinking over something I need to do, while Mike is sleeping, sometimes gently snoring away quite happily.

CHAPTER 43

Jamaican Holiday

With the weekend behind us, it was back to everyday routine. Sometime later, a friend said she was going to visit her sister in Jamaica, and she was sure that her sister wouldn't mind if we came too. A phone call to her said that, yes, she would be delighted to see us as well. She had recently had a big house built and could fit us in quite comfortably. So it was with excitement and happiness that we would be flying off to my home country with our friends Merle and Jerry. (Unfortunately both have since passed away.)

We flew from Manchester, and with a ten-hour journey ahead of us, we settled down to reading, watching the in-flight films, and sleeping. Eventually the pilot said, "Please take your seats for landing." We approached Jamaica International Airport.

On landing, when the doors opened, it was like stepping into an envelope of warm air—that wonderful embrace of Jamaica sunshine. And there in the airport, smiling broadly, was Merle's sister ready to take us to where she lived.

When we arrived, we found the house definitely a "wow" factor. It was a very grand and imposing building, standing on a high bank overlooking the road, with steps going up to an impressive front entrance. Stepping inside to the large hallway was a highly polished floor. Everything about the house was spacious, cool, and airy. From the balcony, our bedroom overlooked green hills that swept down to the sea, to a point called Lover's Leap. Perhaps in the past, some unhappy people took the final jump?

A few days later, Merle and I decided to have a mango eating competition. We both loved mangoes, and it seemed a very good idea. We had a large bucket of mangoes, which a kind man had given to us that morning. We took them onto the balcony and started to eat.

Oh! The juicy and fleshy fruit was oozing with sweetness. There's nothing like a Jamaican mango to get the taste buds going. Mango after mango was devoured with great smacking of lips and juice running down our palms. Five mangoes went down easily, and Merle was on her sixth. I was getting very full. I pushed in another, making it six, while Merle was on her seventh. I was struggling now and managed another, making it seven. Merle was slowing up but still ahead now on eight. That was it. I admitted defeat, while she went on to finish with a glorious ninth. Going back to my room, I gave out a tremendous burp and felt ready for another round. But it was too late, as Merle was declared the "Mango Monarch".

I remember another time that centred on mangoes, when we all went up to Merle's mother property. There, all round her house, were many mango trees. Well, imagine our delight to see this very ripe soft fruit, so juicy and plump,

just waiting to be picked. There were some young boys nearby, and we asked them if they could climb the trees for us and give them a good shake, making the mangos fall to the ground. With big smiles the boys were quickly in the branches and shaking the trees with lots of energy. Very soon it was raining mangoes. Oh! Such happiness as we ran from one mango to another, seeing them fall. We were like kids in a sweet shop where sweets were given out free. We couldn't decide which one to pick up. As one fell, the one beside it looked even riper and better than the one we had just collected. Mike said we would be in the local paper—'Danger! Most wanted women'—for stripping the entire stock of mangoes from the north coast of Jamaica!

We also took a few days down in the capital where Merle's friend lived and had asked her friend, Donald, if he could show us around some of the local beauty spots, from the beach to the markets and other places of interest. We took a trip into the foothills of the Blue Mountains to a place that had formerly been a military hill station for the British Army; it was now a training centre for the Jamaica Defence Force. The idea of the hill station was first raised by the governor general in 1841 because so many soldiers were dying of yellow fever on the plains of Kingston. On average every two and a half days a soldier would die, and the cooler climate at Newcastle reduced the deaths dramatically. (I read that bit out of an information pack I had come across.) Mike had trained up there when stationed in Jamaica, and so it was of great interest to him.

We were in the region where Blue Mountain coffee is grown; the area was cool and misty with lots of rainfall, so the climate and soil was ideal for this famous worldwide

coffee. It was used mainly as a base for nearly all other coffees and was very expensive. We did enjoy a genuine Blue Mountain coffee in a local coffeehouse, where the beans were picked, dried, and ground straight from the side of the mountain we were on.

Leaving Kingston, we were back up to Merle's sister place to find that the goat that she kept had given birth to two little kids. They were sweet little things, still very unsteady on their legs. Both were black and already had been given names. One was Merle and the other was named for me, Lilly May. To this day, I am not sure if we were being called old goats or if it was an expression of affection. I would like to think it was affection.

On one of our trips around the island, we came across a place called the Battle of Rio Nueve, which took place in June 1698. It was the last battle the Spanish fought against the English and the turning point in deciding who would claim possession of the island. The Spanish forces lost and fled to Cuba, while the Jamaicans who sided with them escaped into the mountains and fought a long guerrilla war against the English. So from that time on, English was the spoken word. And Jamaica was ruled by the British Empire, which at the time was still using slaves to work the sugar and tobacco plantations, as was the custom of most of the European countries.

CHAPTER 44

Another Wedding

Then it was time for home and back to cold old Britain, with grey skies and squally weather. We had experienced some wonderful times and happy memories on our holiday and had lots of photographs to show the family. Now it was wedding fever again. This was for our youngest daughter, Marie, all grown up and ready to leave the home at age 20; she was ready to take on the world! And she was ready to start life with her fiancé, Donald.

That would be all three of our children left home, and as parents, we had to let them follow their own destinies. Like all mums and dads, we did miss them. Marie and Donald were married at the Salvation Army Hall in Oakengates. The wedding photos were taken in the local park on a dry but windy day, with the ladies hanging onto their hats and the bride and bridesmaids hanging onto their long flowing gowns.

The reception was at the Great Hay Hotel and Golf Course. I found out that, centuries ago, priory monks used

the land as an enclosure for deer called a *hayye*, a word shortened to *hay* in later years. The hotel was reputed to be haunted, which added an extra mystic atmosphere to the building. It was another successful reception, where the staff as very attentive, the speeches well read, and the meal excellent.

We said goodbye to Marie and Donald as they went off on their honeymoon to the Isle of Man, and now our house was quiet and empty.

It was not to stay quiet for long. Soon we had grandchildren coming to our house. Starting with the children of our son and his wife, whose names were John and Norman. They are all grown up and adults in their own right with their own children and presenting us with grandchildren and great-grandchildren. A neighbour directly across from our house said before he died, "I saw your house being built in the 1940s and early '50s. Since that time, there have always been children running around in your place." It was so true. Even today we have great-grandchildren to keep us company and fill the house with loud squeals of delight and laughter.

Our family, from the youngest to the eldest, have shown us so much love and joy. We feel so blessed. I mentioned earlier on about the Salvation Army. That is where we worship. But at that time, our hall/building had become too small for our Sunday services and other activities that the army did.

CHAPTER 45

Fundraising

For a long time, there had been plans to enlarge our hall or go ahead and build a new and bigger one. There were many meetings on how to raise funds. The new incoming army officer (vicar) sat a meeting and swept aside all the previous building plans, some going back twenty years or more, and said, "Right. We will start from scratch; let's see how much money we can raise."

Various projects were put forward, from coffee mornings to social evenings, but there was nothing like enough to raise the amount needed for a new building. My contribution was slightly different from others, as I volunteered to cook in people's homes. The person was to buy the ingredients, or I would buy it for them and then cook the meal where they lived. I would give them the receipts for the items I had brought. And they would reimburse me for my time cooking and give a donation for the building.

Well, I didn't realise how successful my plan would become. With Mike's help, we went to many houses. The

people always asked for Caribbean-style cooking, so that I had to buy and cook all the ingredients, which could be fried rice Jamaica style, fried chicken, curried chicken, roast potatoes, vegetables, gravy, yams, and sweet potatoes, pork, and sometimes curried goat. Dessert could be trifle done in a special Jamaican way, apple strudel, fresh fruit salad, apple pie, and custard. We had orders from far and wide; the furthest was in Scotland at Gretna Green or south to London. My poor car didn't know what was happening, as we clocked up mile after mile, going from place to place.

The donations were flowing in. Others, too, were busy raising finances, and slowly our building fund was growing. We had some good news from one particular company, who promised to match the money we'd made. That was a tremendous boost to our morale, as well as practical help.

One person came to us, asking if we catered for weddings, which we did not. She explained that the caterer for her daughter's wedding had gone off sick, and it was too late to arrange another one, as the wedding was only two weeks away. So we agreed to help her. What had we let ourselves in for? We had to cater for 150 for the wedding reception and 200 for the evening reception. For days, I was preparing the food in big containers. I spent hours peeling piles of potatoes, as well as cooking a huge number of chicken legs in large saucepans. No Jamaican dinner would be complete without our national dish of rice and peas, so that had to be prepared. There were many Jamaican and Caribbean guests at the wedding.

And English guests had to be catered for as well. I was making fresh fruit salad into the early morning of the wedding itself. Half the food was cooked where we lived

and half at the person's house where the reception was being held. This was in a big marquee in their garden. Trying to keep meals hot was a major problem when we were at the house, as the cooker was a normal standard family cooker plus a microwave and a heating trolley. I still wonder how we managed it. I am not blaming the people whose wedding we were catering for, just pointing out the situation we were in. There were other people there who were waiters and waitresses; otherwise, we would not have succeeded serving and cooking.

When the empty plates and dishes were coming back, Mike spent hours washing up in a normal domestic sink. There were no rubber gloves. So after a while, his hands were all wrinkled with the constant hot water and washing-up liquid.

Then it was repeated all over again for the evening party. We came away from there absolutely drained and almost dropping on our feet. That finished us, and we said no more Caribbean cooking. Our money raising effort was finished, but we had contributed a considerable amount towards our building.

CHAPTER 46

A Little More Cooking

Actually, my cooking experiences were not quite over. I remember that a schoolteacher friend of ours, who knew of our fundraising effort, mentioned that her class was doing a project learning all about the Caribbean. Could I give a talk to the class all about the life in Jamaica, the climate, the countryside, the cooking, the schooling, and any other subject the children might ask about? Always happy to tell others of my home country, I agreed and said I could also do a little Jamaican cooking to give the children a taste of our local food. Our friend was delighted, and it was arranged so that I could use the school kitchen as well.

The day I turned up, I was introduced as Lilly May and looked down at a class of young fresh expectant faces all waiting for me to start. The lesson was a complete success. I think it was the Jamaican cooking that did the trick, as they all had a little taste of johnnycakes (like a dumping, only fried); chicken done in a style used in the Caribbean; Jamaican fried rice; hard dough bread; and Mango juice.

The word got around to other schools, and I was asked or invited to talk and cook for them. It was lovely talking to these young people who were so enthusiastic and willing to learn. At each school, I somehow managed to do a little cooking, as well as giving a talk about my country. I felt so blessed that I was given the chance to tell of my schooling, so completely different from today's education system.

The children were asked to write down what they thought of the cooking and the talks about the Caribbean. I still have their letters of thanks, which to me is a wonderful memory of those times I spent at the different schools, some very touching and some very funny. The innocence of younger children was very refreshing, and they had not been too affected by the cynical attitude of older teenagers growing up in today's world, with the many pressures that surround them.

Flying Lessons

Mike came home one evening telling me about his friend who had found an unusual present for his wife. It was a chance to drive a Lamborghini around a racetrack at high speed. Or she could drive a tank or spend a night in a haunted castle. There were options for other sort of activities that were unusual. He said to me, "Fancy driving a fast car?" Laughing, and as a joke, I said, "I would rather fly a plane."

Time passed, and one day Michael handed me a red envelope and said, "Surprise, surprise." Wondering what it could be, I opened the letter and found he had booked me a flying lesson at a small airport near Wolverhampton Airport.

"A Flying lesson," I said. I was at loss as to what else to say. Mike said, "It's for your Mother's Day present, and it will be different."

For days I was thinking about this flying lesson, and then the day arrived. The whole family came to see me take to the skies. Arriving at Halfpenny Green Airport, I checked in and found my pilot was an older man who was very calm

and pleasant to talk to. He walked me to the plane, which seemed to get larger and larger; he did his safety checks, explaining about the different parts of the plane that had to be inspected.

As I was climbing into the cockpit, I kept thinking to myself. *What on earth am I doing here?*

It was too late now, as I was strapped in to my seat. He described the control panel in front of me. And then he radioed the tower for lift-off. We were sitting side by side, and he was telling me what to do. Slowly at first, the plane taxied onto the runway. We gathered speed, and then faster and faster, we sped down the tarmac. With a roar, the engine increased in volume as I pulled the joystick towards me. Then suddenly, the plane was airborne and soared in to the air.

At first, I could see nothing but blue sky, as the nose was still pointing upwards, and we climbed higher and higher until we levelled out. And there below me was the Staffordshire and Shropshire countryside looking like a patchwork of green, yellow, and brown fields and stretching into a blue and misty distance. In a passenger plane, the countryside below seems so remote and faraway, but in this small plane only a few thousand feet in the air, everything seemed much closer and more personal.

With the instructor by my side and telling me to turn left or right, I felt totally relaxed and was enjoying my experience. We flew over part of Birmingham, turned north, and flew over Wolverhampton and then the town of Telford onto the village of Much Wenlock and started back to the airport.

He said, "As you approach the runway, ease up on the

controls. Keep the plane level and in the middle of the runway. You are doing fine."

Lowering the nose to meet the landing field, I saw the ground get closer and closer, it seemed quicker and quicker. And with a slight bump, we were down.

"Well done, Mrs Green. You've taken off and landed the plane yourself. You have natural flying ability. Would you consider some more lessons?"

I laughed and said, "I don't think I will ever get a chance to fly my own plane."

He laughed and said, "Okay."

The whole experience took just over the hour, and I must say that was a Mother's Day surprise I never expected but thoroughly enjoyed. Mike and the family were there at the side of the terminal building, all waving and pleased that I was still in one piece. When they'd watched the plane come down, they'd thought it was the instructor who had landed it, as it seemed to be a perfect three-point landing. And they were very surprised to learn it was me.

I thought this was a good opportunity to get the same Father's Day present for Mike. He did say his experience was very much the same as mine, except when he came in to land. He landed right on the outer edge of the runway, and the instructor said, "You have miles of runway left. Take off and land, again and again and again." So to the family watching, all thought Mike was bouncing down the landing strip and were rolling about with laughter.

Another surprise we had was on holiday in Scotland. We were staying with a friend at Gretna Green, and we visited the famous blacksmith shop where marriages take place when people elope or run away together. We were looking

around the building and were surprised by the number of minor royals who had come away to be married at Gretna Green. A beautiful young girl, Italian I think, and a very handsome young man came in to the shop. She was in a full bridal gown, and he in a kilt and dress uniform.

They were going to get married, so we quickly made our way to the door to allow the ceremony take place, when they stopped us and asked if we could be witness to their wedding. Both Mike and I were in tracksuits and trainers, hardly dressed for weddings. But they just wanted two people to certify that the wedding was legal and to sign the register. I do not think there are many people who've attended a wedding in tracksuits and trainers.

Our Ghana Experience

Back from holiday, we were in our Army hall and playing in our Salvation Army band when I looked up and saw a young dark boy come into the hall. I thought to myself, I will go and say hello after the meeting. But when the meeting ended, I looked towards where he had been sitting, and he was gone!

The next week was the same. As soon as the morning meeting had finished, the boy was nowhere to be seen. *Right,* I thought. *If he is here next week, I will make sure I meet him before he goes.*

Sure enough, he was there. This time, I rushed straight to the door and caught him on the way out. I invited him to a cup of tea or coffee, as we always had after the morning meeting.

He agreed, and we found out he was from Ghana and studying over here. His name was Emanon. The friendship developed, and soon we were inviting him for Sunday lunch.

One week, he was all excited, saying his father was

in the United Kingdom and coming up to see him. He did eventually arrive, and we invited him along with his son for Sunday lunch. We soon found out that he was a Minister for Health, dealing mainly in Africa and South American countries with AIDS programmes. In the course of conversations, he mentioned that the school in his village was in a dreadful state of disrepair, with big holes in the roof and no toilets for the young people, and they had to walk miles to get water from the river, as the village pump was broken and was beyond repairing.

Now at that time, our corps (Salvation Army) was looking around for a project to help people who were in distress or needed help in other ways. This seemed an ideal opportunity to meet the needs of the school and the village. So Mike started the project rolling by printing maps of Ghana and the area. He included information on the district the school was in, the type of animals that were in the forests and jungles, and the sort of cereals and cooking the local people did. There were lots of information leaflets on the suffering of these poor children in this village. He got photographs of the school (built in 1942)—and how dilapidated it looked—and pictures of children carrying heavy cans of water on their heads to take back to their village some five kilometres distance. He produced a can and filled it with bricks to make people realise how heavy the weight of water they had to carry along dusty and dirt tracks was. The water was not very clean, and in the high summer it would be reduced to a trickle.

The situation seemed to touch a sympathetic nerve with the whole corps, and in a short time, moneymaking projects were under way. From baking cakes to jumble sales,

coffee mornings to holding concerts and cleaning cars to sponsored walks, nearly everyone was doing something for the children and villagers in the district where the school and village stood.

As these money-raising projects were going on, we had an invitation to visit Ghana from Emanon's father and stay with them for two weeks. We thought it would be the ideal opportunity to deliver the money, which had been given to the Salvation Army and held until it was ready to give to the Salvation Army over in Ghana. It would save the money being sent through the Ghanaian Ministry of Education, who would have taken a percentage of the funds raised or other organisations that would have taken their own cut as well.

We were very pleased with the money raised, which had seemed to flow in and came to £7,000—or in Ghanaian currency it was 93,553,890 cedis (pronounced /cee-dees/). Not only was there money; practical items had also been donated. There were exercise books, notebooks, notepads, rulers, erasers, scissors, and biros (very smart executive ones given by a firm), along with complete football strips for the boys and combs and bracelets for the girls. There was a cornet for the Salvation Army band and a tenor horn donated by Mike and myself, and an electric typewriter for the headmaster. Also, there was drawing paper, coloured paper, and other useful things for the school.

Now the difficult part was, how could the corps (church) get a heavy parcel across to Ghana? Luckily, the difficulty was solved by one of the ladies in the corps who worked in a freight department and would ship it over to Ghana for cost price. She and her husband would pay for the shipping.

With that problem solved, we accepted the invitation of Mr Kyrematan, Emanon's father), and a date was fixed for us to fly over (at our own expense). So from a small beginning of just saying hello had now grown this major project. We left in late June and settled down for the nearly nine-hour flight to Accra (Ghana's capital city and main airport).

The flight was uneventful, and then we were fastening our seat belts for landing in Ghana. We cleared customs, and there to meet us, smiling broadly, was Mr Kyrematan. He drove us to his house, and that in itself was an experience. Once off the main motorway, there were so many potholes in the local streets his four-wheel drive people carrier was swerving all over the road in an effort to miss them. At the same time, other drivers were driving in a similar fashion, all driving towards the one undamaged part of the road.

Arriving at his house, his wife, Hanna, and family were there to welcome us. We soon settled in and, the next day, were off to the Accra airport's customs clearance building to collect our parcel sent over a week earlier. We waited and waited and hung around.

Eventually, Mr Kyrematan produced his Member of Parliament identification pass and demanded to see where our container was. This stirred up officials, who were then scurrying around to find it. When it finally arrived, it had been opened. Missing were the complete football strip for the boys, some notebooks and notepads, some scissors and rulers, plus some clothes we had brought for the local officer's little boy. We think the officials had deliberately made us wait around so we would bribe them in order to get the box.

A few days later, we were to present the cheque and items to the school. This was in the village where Mr

Kyrematan (Kwisi was his first name) grew up as a boy. When we arrived, there was an excited crowd to see us. All the children had the day off school for this occasion. So with lots of shouts and cheers, we were all led in to a big hall. We were asked to sit on the platform, along with other officials and local dignitaries, and from our raised view, we were looking over a huge sea of faces. We were welcomed in by many speeches, all of which we could not understand, as they were in the Ashanti dialect, and we had two little girls who danced in front of us and welcomed us in carefully rehearsed English, which was very touching.

It was our turn to present the cheque of the huge-sounding amount of 93,553,890 cedis. There was an enormous roar and clapping from the people, and then it was their turn to shower us with gifts of woodcarvings and national colourful costumes.

Kwisi then started to show the people what had been collected for the school, amid more roars of approval. But the biggest noise was from the children as they yelled, cheered, clapped, and jumped up and down when they were told that the executive biros were for them, not their parents, and that they could use them for school and homework.

With the welcoming ceremony over, we were then led out to see the school and the village. The newer school buildings were in reasonable condition, but the one that had been built in 1942 really showed its age. It was now used as the infants' school, and we were told it had never been repaired. It was a long low building with a thatched roof. Sides of the building had been eaten by beetles and were crumbling away. There were open windows, with no glass to keep out the flies and other insects, no ceiling fans

to cool the air down, and many floorboards missing—in some cases just dirt floors and no toilet facilities. The roof was very threadbare, letting in rain. When that happened, the children had to move to a drier part of the school. Even the headmaster's office was outside under an extension of the roof. So it was time for a complete rebuild.

We also visited other school buildings, where the children had made their way back to their own classes after the ceremonies were over. For me, it was like reliving, back in time, my own school days of large classes and a sea of brown faces.

That same day, we were to travel to the village of Kyesherwere deep in the interior of the Kumasi District, and the ride seemed to go on for ages. We eventually got there, and there was a big cheer from the children but not from the adults, who had been waiting for us for nearly three hours or more.

It was like stepping into a film set. The village was a mixture of thatched roofs and more modestly built houses, circling the village square. Two heavy chairs were set out under an awning for us to watch the ceremonies. Speeches and dances were performed on the square in our honour. Money was given for a water pump to be installed in the village, and the assemblyman (second in command to the chief) gave out the local news and told the villagers that, when the second pump was installed and working, the children would not have to queue for water at a waterhole some three miles away but go to school instead.

There were murmurs of disagreement, as it was the children's normal job to collect the water, feed the chickens and pigs, sweep the house, and then go to school. It reminded

me of my life as a little girl, when some of my school friends had to do similar chores.

The day finally ended, and we made our way back to Kwisi's house, having seen and experienced real village life in Ghana. A few days later, Mr Kyrematan took us sightseeing around different places of interest in the Kumasi region. The first one was Kakum National Park—375 kilometres of virgin rain forest leading in to the central region of Ghana. We were taken to treetop walkways high up in the trees and challenged to walk across these rather wobbly narrow fraying rope bridges some 70 metres (200 feet) high. It reminded me of the TV programme *I'm a Celebrity … Get Me out of Here!* There were eight of these walks, which we did, and I felt very pleased with myself as I do not like heights.

Our next outing was to a very large, thought-to-be extinct volcano now filled with water. We were asked if we would like a trip around the lake, to which we said yes. We were sitting in the boat, when all of a sudden, lots of young people appeared from nowhere. They scrambled onto the boat before it cast off from the water's edge. Mike was saying, "Wait a minute. I am not paying for all these as well, am I?"

But it turned out that you hired the boat and not the passengers, so they jumped in to the craft and scrounged a free boat ride. Probably they had done it many times with unsuspecting visitors.

Days passed, and we were off to a crocodile farm in the Cape Coast area. There were wooden walkways over the crocodile pond so you could look down into the water and see many long heavy crocodiles with their snouts or noses, whatever you call them, just above the water. They

were slowly swimming towards us in the hope of catching a chicken leg that we were eating.

We were fascinated by the very noisy Weaverbirds at the pond while we were having a coffee. They were busy in the trees just above our heads constructing their nests and weaving straw, grass, and small bendy twigs with their beaks, intertwining them into a ball and shaping the nests they were building. It was intriguing to watch.

It was arranged that we would meet with the district commissioner in that area. Driving up to his very palatial house, we were met by two policemen, who checked us into the house. There we met the commissioner, who was sitting in an armchair with his foot resting on a stool. After exchanging introductions and small talk, I asked him what was wrong with his foot.

He laughed and said he'd had a small operation on it. Then turned to Kwisi and said, "I think she is an Ashanti?" Kwisi said, "I thought that the moment I met her."

Apparently, the Ashanti people are very bold and warlike and had many battles with the English from the 1900s to the early twentieth century. So who knows? Perhaps my ancestry started in Ghana. Thousands of slaves were shipped out to British colonies in the 1700s. (I looked that bit up.) Ghanaian women seemed rather meek and mild and tended to follow their husband's orders or advice. With Mike and myself, whatever came up, it was invariably a joint decision.

Who knows? Perhaps I will follow it up to see if my origins started there. We were taken to a cocoa research station and saw people sorting out the cocoa beans. They would start first by breaking open the outer husk of the beans and then drying them in the sun and finally sorting

out the good from the bad beans. We also found out there were other products made from the cocoa bean—butter, cream, shampoo, jam marmalade, chocolate powder, and fertiliser.

Kwisi had a phone call one morning saying there was a three-line whip in Parliament and so he had to go, as his presence would be important to carry the vote Parliament was putting through. So with him looking very smart in his suit, Hanna in her best dress, myself in a pink flowing dress, and Mike complete in collar and tie, we all went to the Houses of Parliament, Kwisi off to vote, and us to the visitors' gallery and listening to the proceedings going on down below in the main hall (or forum I think it is called?).

Our time was coming to an end, but Mike and I remembered we had come across a shop that made and sold coffins. It wasn't just ordinary coffins but coffins made to order; if you were a chicken farmer, your coffin could be made into a very lifelike chicken and big enough to carry a body, and it would be painted in the colours of a chicken. It was the same if you were a soldier. You could be buried in a life-sized cannon. We saw a big Bible, which obviously would belong to a preacher. There was a very good likeness of a training shoe. So perhaps the person had been an athlete. It was quite unusual but very interesting.

On our last sightseeing adventure, we had a visit to a castle that was one of the "forty slave castles" built along the coast West of Ghana. It was originally built by the Portuguese as a warehouse to protect their gold trade, but later it became the centre of the Dutch slave trade. Then later it fell into British hands. It was used to hold slaves before they were loaded onto ships to the Americas and the

Caribbean. At the castle, there was a famous gate called "Gate of no Return." This was the last doorway the slaves would see before being shipped off and sent to cotton or sugar plantations. Even after all these years, there still seemed to be a dreadful atmosphere in the dungeons, and it was easy to imagine the squalid and cramped conditions these poor people suffered.

Our guide told us up to 1,000 men and boys and 500 women and girl slaves were shackled and crammed in the castle's dank, poorly ventilated dungeons, with no space to lie down and with very little light. Without water or sanitation, the floor of the dungeons would have been littered with human waste, and many captives fell seriously ill. The men and boys were separated from the women and girls into two holding chambers, and the castle also featured confinement cells—small pitch-black dungeons for prisoners who revolted or were seen as rebellious. They were shut in these cells and left to die—no food, no water—and then the bodies were thrown into the harbour for the sharks.

Once the slaves set foot in the castle, they could spend up to three months in captivity under those dreadful conditions before being shipped off to the New World or the Caribbean. We came away from there feeling depressed and wondering how men could be so inhuman to other men and women. Our last evening with Kwisi and Hanna was an enormous farewell dinner. Every vegetable and fruit of Ghana was there to be tasted. We tried to do our best and demolish this mountain of delicious food, and to finish, I was presented with the biggest mango in the world—or so it seemed!

Oh how I tried to get through this sweet juicy tasty fruit, but I was too full and sorrowfully had to admit defeat and leave part of this wonderfully yummy scrumptious mouth-watering delightful harvest on my plate.

CHAPTER 49

Home Once More

The next day was our flight home, and we were so sorry to leave these generous, kind-hearted people. Although we helped with school improvements and a water pump for a village, we received far more blessings than we gave and came away with precious memories.

Our last memory of Ghana was when we were taken to the airport. We were escorted into the first class lounge, which was worthy of the Ritz or Hilton Hotel, full of armchairs, settees, and thick pile rugs, and there was a bar serving refreshments and drinks. We waited with Kwisi. When it was announced that passengers for flight KL1481 to Birmingham were to proceed to gate number three, we got up to go, but he said, "No, You can wait a bit longer. There's no hurry." So we waited and waited, soon getting anxious about the passing time and the boarding of the aircraft.

Eventually a very smart young lady in uniform came up to us and said, "Mr and Mrs Green, this way please." So

after a hurried goodbye to Kwisi, we followed the stewardess down some stairs, and outside was a coach waiting to take us to the plane. The coach was completely empty except for the two of us. Once in, we sped off right up to the door of the waiting plane.

As soon as we scuttled in to our "economy class" seats, the doors closed, and we were off, leaving lots of annoyed people having to wait and wondering who we were.

CHAPTER 50

The Queen's Garden Party

One day, Mike opened the post, and then a big grin came over his face. "You had better go out and buy another hat," he said. We had received a very official-looking letter from the palace in London, saying:

> *The Lord Chamberlain is commanded by her Majesty to invite Mr and Mrs Green to the Queens Garden party at Buckingham Palace: Morning Dress uniform or lounge suit.*

Now Mike was a civil servant and worked for the Crown, so was entitled to apply. And a certain number of civil servants were accepted each year to attend. What made it more humorous was that Mike's co-worker in the office saw the invitation and suggested they both apply, which they did. Much to his colleague's annoyance, my husband was accepted, while nothing came of his application.

So I was out, dress and hat hunting, while he was looking for a new suit. Actually another friend came to

the rescue for Mike and loaned him his very smart, very expensive pinstriped business suit, complete with waistcoat, which was perfectly fitting for the occasion. I spent a lot of time in shops and eventually found the ideal dress and hat for the garden party. It was a lovely yellow, enhancing my Caribbean colour.

So fully fitted out, we both were ready for the royal occasion ahead. Our plan was to drive down to the town of Reading in West Berkshire; stay overnight with the two wonderful friends who I called Mum and Dad (formerly Captain and Mrs Wick, who managed the Salvation Army School for the Blind in Jamaica); and catch a train to Victoria Station, which was the nearest station to Buckingham Palace. From there, we would take a taxi to the palace.

It did not quite work out that way. When we came off the platform at Victoria and looked for a taxi, there before us was a long trail of top hats, military hats, and women's broad or floppy hats all walking in one direction. We simply followed the hats, and there was Buckingham Palace stretched out before us. Up to the large imposing gates we went and then were directed to a slightly smaller one, where we were checked in by two very large policemen.

Once through, we stepped through another archway and came out looking over a sea of people all milling about on the garden lawn. Parts of the lawn were partitioned off to make way for royalty to walk down. We watched this spectacle for a little while. Court officials walked down these lanes and would stop and ask a person on the other side of the barrier if he or she would like to be introduced to the queen or other royal persons who were there. When the member of the royal household came near, the selected

person would step forward under the barrier, so the queen, prince, and princess could meet him or her.

As we stood no chance of getting to the front of the crowd, we wandered around the gardens for a while. We listened to a military band that was playing on one part of the lawn and came across a long line of marquees, all serving drinks and refreshments. Great! We were both thirsty, and Mike was hungry, so he demolished the largest slice of chocolate cake ever known to man, while I enjoyed a delicate cup of tea courtesy of the queen.

We eventually found a table, and sitting there was a very distinguished-looking gentleman who, in the course of conversation we found out, used to be personal secretary to Winston Churchill. We remarked how young he looked, and he said his secret was working with young musicians at the Mehudi Menuhin School of Music, where he was a director. We also met the general of the Salvation Army and his wife. By this time, everyone was getting excited, as the royal party was making its way into the garden, ready to meet the public.

We knew we did not stand a chance to get closer to the front of the gathering, so settled to peer between or over people's shoulders. A policeman who was at the front saw me struggling to see and said, "Make room for this lady. She's only little."

Grudgingly, people shifted, and I wriggled my way up to the barrier and there had a first-class view of the Princess Diana as she went by. (Mike was still near the back and saw the top of her head.)

The other royals, who we saw at a distance, were the Queen, the Duke of Edinburgh Prince Phillip, and Prince

Charles; and there was Lady Diana, Princess of Wales, very close. On her way back to Kensington Palace, the car she was in swept right past us. I waved to her, and she leant out of the window waving and gave me a very broad smile.

We were extremely lucky with the weather, as it was dry, bright, and sunny. At the previous garden party, we were told there was a torrential rainfall, and many ladies had their high heels stuck in the lawn and their suits or dresses drenched. With the party over, it was time to go back. So again following the top hats and ladies in their many varieties of hats, we made our way back to Victoria Railway Station and then onto Reading. It was a very colourful and exciting day for Michael and me.

It was now high summer, and the days were warm, the skies were blue, and the winds were light breezes. All the windows were open in our Salvation Army hall. Our Sunday morning congregation was slightly less than normal, as some were away on holiday. But we could see we had a few visitors, and it was our policy to try and make people welcome. So after the service was over, we introduced ourselves and spoke to a couple who was looking around the hall. We found out that they had come all the way from New Zealand and were staying at a cottage that was a World Heritage site along the River Severn. They too were in the Salvation Army, and their corps was in near a place that was famous for its opencast gold-mining and the largest mine in New Zealand.

We said our goodbyes, and off we went to get ready for our families, who always came to us for Sunday dinner. The following Sunday, the pair from New Zealand was at our morning service. Again we struck up a conversation with the couple and found out that their names were Sheila and Jim

and they were going home on Friday. I had a ladies meeting on Tuesday, and it was to be at our place. There was going to be a barbecue in our garden. I asked, Would they like to come?

They readily accepted and came along with twenty-five of my ladies group and helpers (called the Home League, one of the Salvation Army's women's group). We were blessed with good weather, good food, and good company. Sheila gave a talk on the women's Home League in New Zealand. They left us with the offer that, if ever we came to New Zealand, we were to look them up. We thanked them for their offer, but little did we realise we would be seeing them again.

CHAPTER 51

A Trip Down Under

Time passed, and we had a letter from a friend who had kept in touch with us for many years. It read, 'Hello, you two. I've made your bed; it's ready and waiting for you to fly over and lie in it. All your family have now grown up and married, so you have no excuse not to come to Australia and visit us."

That was true, and she had made the offer many times before. But there had always been something turning up not making it possible. We talked it over and decided to find out what the cost would be. So off to the travel agent we went and made some enquiries.

It seemed promising, but first Mike would have to get time off work. Going that distance, it would take more than a two-week holiday to make the trip worthwhile. By working through his TOIL (Time off In lieu) privilege through the year, having two weeks off his normal entitlement, and taking a week's unpaid leave, he could make it up to four weeks. This was reluctantly agreed to by his manager. So he

was in a position to write back and say we would soon be on our way.

Going back to the travel agent's, we'd started to make arrangements for the flight to Australia, when the girl said, "There are some special deals on at the moment with budget hotels. Why not take in some more countries on your way there and take advantage of the offers? We said we would like to know what the overall cost would be. So the flight would be London to Hawaii, Singapore, Malaya, Australia, New Zealand, and return back to London. The package was affordable, so we set about making plans.

We phoned our friends in Australia (Jenny and Allen who we had met many years ago in Tidworth) and of course our friends in New Zealand, asking if there would be a bed and breakfast place nearby so we could see them. A very quick reply came back, saying they would be delighted to see us again, but we must stay at their place.

We were all excited and told our very good friends Merle and Gerry. Merle said, "Oh that sounds lovely. Can we book up as well?"

Gerry said, "Wait a minute. We need to work out our finances first."

We had to ring back, this time asking about bed and breakfast for our two friends.

Jenny and Allen rang back, saying, "It is not a problem, as we have plenty of rooms. We can fit your friends in easily." It was the same with our friends in New Zealand, Jim and Sheila: "You and your friends must stay with us." and with typical humour, Jim added, "Then if you don't like our place, we can always direct you to a bed and breakfast in the town."

So it was on a bright October morning, bags packed and all the necessary visas and passports checked, that Mike and I and Merle and Gerry were off on our trip to Hawaii. I always thought Hawaii was an island, but it is a chain of islands in the Pacific Ocean. Of the six main islands, Oahu has Hawaii's biggest city and capital, Honolulu, home to Waikiki Beach and Pearl Harbour's World War II memorials. The first part of our journey was to Honolulu some fifteen hours flying time away. I cannot remember much of the plane journey; I guess it was long and boring.

Eventually, our plane landed at Honolulu International Airport on Oahu, met by a taxi ready to take us to our hotel. On arrival, we were surprised at the luxurious rooms we were given, all very clean and highly decorated and with lovely views of the beach. Considering this was a "budget hotel," this seemed to be a very good start. After a rest from our journey, we were out exploring the surrounding area and soaking up the sun, hot and burning into our shoulders.

It was very similar to Jamaica—very green, very tropical, blue skies, colourful birds, and people walking around in light and airy clothing. We found Waikiki Beach, famous for its long rolling breakers, making it ideal for professional surfers and beginners alike. We settled on to the beach, watching all the activities that were going on—beach ball, surfing, canoeing, and sunbathing. But after a while, it became too hot and we had to move.

Another day, we explored some of the town, had a tour of the southern part of the island, and listened to some fascinating facts about Honolulu. Finally, we took a tour to Pearl Harbour and learned about the attack on Pearl Harbour, a surprise strike by the Imperial Japanese Navy

Air Service against the United States Naval Base on the morning of 7 December 1941. We were ferried out to the USS *Arizona* Memorial in the harbour, which marks the resting place of 1,102 sailors and marines killed on that ship during the Japanese attack. The USS *Arizona* was hit four times by Japanese bombers and eventually sank. We sailed over the ship and could look down into the placid waters and dimly see the deck and gun turrets of the *Arizona*.

We then continued to a huge memorial floating platform in the harbour, giving the names of all those who were killed, not only on the USS *Arizona* but also of all those who had lost their lives in the battle of Pearl Harbour. It was a very moving experience.

We were in Honolulu for four days. Then it was time to head south and move on to our next stopover, New Zealand, where our friends Jim and Shirley were expecting us. That meant another plane journey and more hours of reading sleeping and eating. Eventually the call to fasten our seat belts came as we approached Auckland International Airport.

With a slight bump, we were down, and it seemed in no time we were through customs and out into the arrivals terminal. There to meet us were Jim and Sheila. After lots of hugs and well wishes, we were off to where they lived. I can't remember how we got there. It must have been by car, but we all felt comfortable, so it probably was a big one.

Jim had big plans for us and wanted to show as much of New Zealand as possible. So the next day, we were ready and off to another extinct volcano filled with water and the Huka Falls, a fast-flowing river and an awesome sight because of the vivid milky blue water of the river and the

sheerness of the gorge. It tumbles into a magnificent wide canyon after a three-metre drop. The roar of the falls and the trembling earth beneath your feet remind you just how powerful the river is. I don't think we will ever forget that site or the largest opencast gold mine in New Zealand.

The next day, we were off to see the enormous hole in the earth, some 1,500 metres around and 250 metres deep; it was a truly impressive place. There was an old Cornish pumping station, which used to pump water out of the mine, right back to 1902—no longer in use of course.

Another memorable place was called (in Maori) Wai-O-Tapu (Sacred Water). With the thermal springs of hot boiling pools of mud, the smell of sulphur was everywhere. We had to be careful where we walked, as there were fumaroles of hissing steam. It was like a glimpse into hell.

We took a trip back up to Auckland to see some of the yachts in the harbour. It was the famous "around-the-world yacht race," and many international boats were in. Quite a few were out of the water, but their hulls were covered up by tarpaulins, so as the opposition could not see what design or shape they were in to gain or steal an advantage for their own yachts.

While we were in Auckland, we had the chance to go up the Sky Tower, the tallest building in New Zealand, which stands at 1,076 feet, or roughly 328 metres. The top part of the tower has two restaurants and a cafe—including New Zealand's only revolving restaurant. We used the observation platform. In one place, there was a glass floor where you could look straight down and see the tiny cars and tinier people all going about their daily business. It was not a good place to be if you suffered from vertigo.

We went to many other places but too many to mention in a book like this. Jim and Sheila were the perfect people to be with, and it was jokes and laughter all through our stay with them.

Sadly, our time ran out, and so it was time to say farewell and be off on our travels once more. From New Zealand, we flew on across Australia to Adelaide, which was right down in the Southern part of the country. It was another long flight journey, some 4,700 miles (8,100) kilometres over the huge expanse of the Pacific Ocean.

We did stop at the tiny island of Tonga for refuelling. Nobody got off the plane, and I remember some very heavy thick-set passengers got on. I was left wondering how they were going to fit in their seats. They were not fat but very broad and sturdy.

We were on the ground for about three-quarters of an hour, and then we were off again. Hours later, we flew over what used to be called Ayers Rock, now known as Uluru—the landmark name used by the local people. A British surveyor, William Gosse, was the first European to "discover" the monolith—the largest rock of its kind in the world—and named it Ayers Rock after the former chief secretary of South Australia, Sir Henry Ayers.

I had a good view as we passed overhead, but all Mike saw were many heads peering out of the windows. Then it was gone. Later, Adelaide came into view, and it was time to fasten our seat belts once more. Adelaide Airport is the main airport in South Australia and the fifth busiest airport in the country (another fact I picked up).

There in the arrivals terminal were Jenny and Alan, her husband, waving to catch our attention. It was all hugs

and smiles after such a long time. It was then into their people carrier and off to their house at North Haven on the outskirts of Adelaide. There was so much to catch up on, as we had not seen them for years and the talking went on late into the night. We were all tired after our long trip. No sooner had we gone to bed, it seemed time to get up again.

We were very lucky with transport; Alan was going to sell his people carrier, but when he knew we and our friends were coming, he decided to wait until after we had gone and then sell it, which was very kind of him. Having the people carrier made it so much easier for all six of us to get around.

Adelaide itself was a busy and modern city with all the top shops on hand. Broad streets and boulevards are everywhere, with plenty of parks. The weather was on the cool side, as it was just coming in to their spring. Jenny and Alan decided to take us on a trip right up to the edge of the outback, and we travelled through many sleepy villages on our way to a place once famous for its gold fields. We stopped overnight in motels, and then on to the old gold diggings.

We found out there was a rebellion in 1854. Gold miners in the town of Ballerat revolted against the high prices of mining licences. The local police contingent had been joined by soldiers from the British Army to stop the protestors. Jenny and Allen took us there where the local people re- enacted the protests and riots, which took place and were brutally put down the demonstrating miners, with violence and viciousness.

From there, we went on to another discovery of gold in Bendigo during the 1850s, which made it one of the most significant Victorian boomtowns in Australia. News

of the finds increased the gold rush, bringing thousands of migrants to the city from around the world.

Another place we visited was an old-fashioned one-street town called the Mulberry Settlement, set in the 1850s. On the main street, tin coffins were on display, propped up against shop walls and mannequins put inside them representing dead people. People walked around dressed in the period of the time. Old-fashioned penny-farthing bicycles were pedalled around the street. Barbers were shaving customers outside their shops with the old-fashioned cut-throat razors. Women were sweeping their front porches with besom brooms of the time. There were lots of children in the town from a nearby school, and they were about to watch a protest march for Votes for Women. A man came up to us and asked if we would like to join in the march, and we agreed. First we had to change into heavy skirts and blouses of the day. Merle, Jenny, and I marched with the other women, shouting, "Votes for women," and, "Ban the bra," which I'm sure wasn't in the script, but we thoroughly enjoyed it. All the children were cheering and shouting, and they too were enjoying the protest.

Another trip was down the Murray River, the longest river in Australia on a paddle steamer. Again it was a step back into a distant past. As we slowly glided by fields, trees, and houses, it seemed like we were in a different world, where everything was in slow time, and a feeling of calm relaxation came over us all.

With our adventures coming to an end, we were making our way back to Adelaide. Mike said to Alan, "Do you know, Alan, we have driven all this way and we haven't seen one kangaroo yet?" "Leave that to me," said Alan.

As we were nearing Adelaide, he took a side turn, and we ended up in a wildlife park. There before us were kangaroos, koala bears, Tasmanian devils, wombats, and other animals. Trying to photograph a koala bear is an amusing challenge. We tried to photograph a koala bear hugging a tree, and he simply turned his face away. We ran round the other side of the tree, and he turned his face away again. We tried this several times, but each time he would look the other way. In the end, we gave up and left him in peace.

Back to Adelaide, and it was time to say goodbye to Janet and Alan, who had looked after us so well. We were taking with us memories of a very interesting journey, which we still vividly remember even today.

Our next stop was Malaya and then on to Singapore. We turned north and took the flight up to Kuala Lumpur—this time, only just over seven hours. As before, on arrival, we were looking for a taxi to take us to our budget hotel, which was somewhere off Orchard Road, a famous street of Kuala Lumpur! There were beautiful walk-throughs between shopping malls and food outlets. You could step into any of the huge malls with all the known brands under one roof.

Our hotel could easily compete with our British-priced, four- and five-star hotels back in the United Kingdom. Spotlessly clean, spacious rooms, very polite staff, and we were very near the city centre for sightseeing and for Merle and me to do a little bit of shopping. There was colourful Chinatown, a bargain hunter's paradise that seemingly never slept. The streets were always busy, no matter what time of day or night.

We made a trip up to Malacca by bus. Gerry and Merle did not come, as Gerry was not feeling very well. Malacca

is or was famous for its cane or walking sticks made of an East Indian rattan palm. But there seemed a dark air of depression over the town, as there were many black flags flying from different houses, proclaiming their allegiance to Islam. We did not feel comfortable in the town and were glad to get on the bus again. I think that was the only downside we had during our whole trip.

Our days were coming to an end, as we packed and made our way to the airport and ready for our flight to Singapore. This was the shortest flight, taking only an hour and a half to Changi Airport. Again we looked for a taxi to our hotel. When we arrived, it could have been the Dorchester or the Ritz. It looked so exclusive, with marble floors, hanging chandeliers, statues in every corner, glass mirrors from wall to ceiling, and porters in smart uniforms. And the showpiece was a sweeping golden double staircase leading up to more floors.

By this time Gerry was feeling quite weak and low. We didn't know it at the time, but he was suffering from cancer and got tired very quickly.

The next day we decided to go sightseeing and, from our hotel, strolled down to a milling throng of people all busy going about their everyday lives. The streets were very colourful, and the smell of spices drifted through the air. Our claim to fame in Singapore was visiting the famous colonial-style luxury hotel named after British statesman Sir Thomas Raffles, the founder of Singapore. To stay there, you have to be very wealthy. We were having a taxi sightseeing journey around the town and were bursting for the toilet. The taxi stopped outside the hotel, and Merle and I ran in

and used their very plush, highly decorated bathroom—Oh! What a relief—and then ran out again.

A day or two later, we had booked a sightseeing boat trip around Singapore Harbour but saw nothing through the torrential and driving rain, just vague outlines of very tall buildings through the pouring walls of water hammering down and bouncing high off the deck of the boat. One of Mike's sayings was, "You win some, and you lose some." That afternoon was a definite loss.

The next day, the sun was at its best, so we decided to do some last-minute shopping before we left for the United Kingdom. Gerry did not come, as he was feeling very tired. Leaving him in his room, we strolled down to the market. After our shopping, we made a leisurely stroll back to our hotel, to find that Gerry wasn't there. Merle was very worried, thinking he had been taken to hospital. We phoned down to reception. No ambulance had been called, and there was no sign of him.

CHAPTER 52

A Missed Flight

Time passed, and then suddenly Gerry appeared and said he was feeling a little better, so he slipped out to buy a present for a young boy we all knew at church who came from a poor neighbourhood. He then said, "By the way, we should have been at the airport this morning, and our flight has long gone. The cleaners came in to change our sheets for the next incoming occupants and wondered why we had not checked out."

We were horrified. How could this be? It turned out, every flight we had taken had always been on a Monday, but this flight was on a Sunday. Now here in Singapore, we were some nearly 7,000 miles (10,888 kilometres) from the United Kingdom. The airline booking office was closed, so we were advised by the reception desk to go to the airport tomorrow and see if there were any spare seats.

I was thinking, *Oh well! Another day in the tropics.* The others were quite concerned, especially for Gerry, who was steadily getting worse. I don't think they slept very well

over the worry of getting back home. I just said, "Lord, we place this problem into your hands, so *you* deal with it, as you always do."

The next day came, and we checked out of the hotel and down to the airport. We explained to the girl at the check-in desk how the mix-up had occurred, and she went through her computer looking for seats.

Great! She found four remaining spare seats, and booked us in. The wonderful thing was that we did not have to pay anything extra. And so we ended an amazing holiday and flew north, back up to London.

On arrival at Heathrow Airport, there was Merle's son waiting to pick them up and his friend following behind to bring us back as well. Gerry was now very weak, so Merle had phoned ahead, asking their son to collect him. A few days later, he was admitted to hospital and, sadly, never came out. It was a hard time for Merle, and it took her a long time to get over his loss, as they were very close together.

The months went by, and we slipped into our normal everyday routine. Our holiday was now a dim, distant memory.

CHAPTER 53

On Our Travels Again

Mike came from work telling me he was to be awarded the Imperial Service Medal for services to the crown. He had served twenty-five years with Her Majesty's Forces and now as a civil servant a further twenty-five years, and he was coming up for retirement. The medal presentation ceremony was to be held at the barracks in Shrewsbury, and the entire family was invited.

The medal was presented by Major General Morton in front of a large crowd, which was a total surprise to Mike, who thought it would be a low-key affair. It was nice that we, as a complete family, were there to see the presentation and, afterwards, enjoy coffee and refreshments in the officers' mess. We felt very proud of him.

It was not long after that Mike's time as a civil servant was coming to an end—or so we thought. He was asked to stay on for a further year, working in Shrewsbury on a part-time basis. He was quite happy to do so, for his main

worry was that he did not want to vegetate once his work had finally finished.

That only lasted a year, as the whole organisation was moved down to Bulford in Wiltshire. He was still fit and active so started to look around for further employment. A few months later, an opportunity appeared working in an office that dealt with people who got caught for drinking whilst driving. The police would advise the offender to contact the company, who would send the wrongdoer on a drink driver awareness scheme in or near his or her town or city. Instead of paying a speeding fine, he or she would pay the company for the awareness course. In most cases, it seemed to work very well.

Mike worked there for a further five years and was very content and happy with the staff and managers. Again, the company was just around the corner from where we lived. The staffs were mainly young, and he was looked upon as granddad, but they respected him, as he too respected them. His job changed several times within the company, and he ended up sorting out the mail, which flowed like a river through the office.

On his farewell he was presented with a beautiful engraved silver pen from the bosses and a lovely carriage clock from the staff. In a way, he was sorry to go but felt after all the years apart we had experienced that it was time to be together, and we could plan and explore what we wanted to do in each other's company.

We still had the travel itch as a result of all the different moves we had whilst Mike was in the army, and I, like him, never got over the urge to travel to new or unusual places.

We now had more leisure time and could book and travel to distant places—well, as far as our pockets would allow us.

There was always Majorca, as our daughter Aline had now settled on the island she and her husband ran a business together. So it was a yearly visit to their place and to spend time with them.

Another fascinating place we visited was the island of Nisyros, not far from Kos, one of the Greek islands famous for its volcano. It is a place where you can actually walk on the crust of the volcano. When it erupted, the magma was hurled in to the air but fell straight down back into the crater from where it was ejected. It cooled and hardened in places like a rice pudding forming a skin. But it was still a dangerous place to be, as fumaroles and hot gases were being forced up through the outer layer of the crust. We were told to wear sensible shoes, as the floor was still very warm in places and not to wear flip-flops or sandals. Our guide was talking to us when she stepped backwards at the same time boiling hot steam gushed out from the fumarole behind her and scalded her heel and back of her leg. We were so sorry for her, as it must have been very painful.

The crater seemed like a giant cereal bowl, with people's houses built on the rim. We found it odd to have buildings erected in such a precarious position, where mini eruptions and minor earthquakes still happened from time to time.

Final Trip around the World

I suppose the final urge to travel culminated in our second trip around the world, which we had planned for a long time. We flew from London again using the "budget hotel" system staying for a few days in each location. We flew with Cathay Pacific, and there were some lovely-looking stewardesses moving up and down the aisle. Every time one passed by our seats, Mike would nudge me and say, "Ooooh. I'm in love!" as they gave him a smile.

Our first stop was Bangkok, and that was for three nights. While we there, we took a coach trip to the bridge over the River Kwai—made famous of course by the film *The Bridge on the River Kwai*—and a short ride on the "Death Railway". We were told that about 9,000 Allied soldiers had lost their lives through brutal treatment of the Japanese soldiers and many jungle diseases that infected the camps along the railway.

In one of the monasteries, we saw a huge five-ton golden Buddha that had an interesting history. When the Japanese

overran the country in 1941, the monks started burying and hiding their statues of Buddha; the one we saw was disguised and hidden not too far from the monastery. The monks covered the statue in concrete, and there it stayed for years. Eventually, the religious community either moved away or fled from the oncoming Japanese advance, and so it was left and ignored as a concrete statue, and the jungle claimed back the area. Years passed, the war had ended, and the ground was going to be cleared to make way for a car park. When the bulldozers moved in, they started to move the statue, but it was raining hard, so they decided to move it in the morning. Come the next day, they saw that the bulldozer had chipped away some of the concrete. There, showing underneath, was a yellow colour. On closer inspection, they realised the statue was made of gold. And a long-lost, long forgotten Buddha had been found which was now in the monastery we visited.

From Bangkok, we flew on to Hong Kong and stayed at a nice hotel in the Wan Chai District, which is well known as the restaurant area of Hong Kong. That night, we set out to have a proper Chinese meal and started looking in all the restaurants along the strip. Trouble was, Hong Kong had recently been handed over to the Chinese from the British, and every menu was written in Chinese, so we could not read any of them. So our claim to fame was eating a Mac Donald's burger from a fast-food takeaway.

We had a guided tour of Hong Kong and Victoria Peak, which Mike had remembered from his army days. Instead of the little hut on Victoria Peak he recalled, there was now a very modern supermarket in its place. There was also Aberdeen, the floating fish markets, where you could get

any type of fish and so fresh; the waiter would scoop the hapless creature of your choice from the aquarium, pop it in the frying pan, and prepare it there and then. We were there for three nights.

Time to move on and our next stop was Bali. That was for five nights. We stayed in a beautiful hotel with mango trees growing up to our balcony. I was delighted, I could see the mangoes; smell the mangoes; and, if I reached out far enough, pick the mangoes. Now there was one particularly plump fleshy one very near our balcony, which I was watching all the time we were there. My plan was to reach out and take it the day we were leaving.

Meanwhile, we watched a Balinese story told in dance style. Balinese dancing is very expressive. The means used to convey expressions are hand and eye movements, which are exaggerated. Eyebrows are lifted, and the eyes glance and roll sideways and down, and in all directions hands flutter and twist.

We visited some rice paddy fields and actually saw for the first time black rice, which didn't look very interesting. We went to a temple built in the sixteenth century and still in use by the monks. We were to visit another active volcano, but the weather turned; we had torrential rain for the day, so the tour was cancelled.

The day we were due to leave, I thought, *now is the time for my mango outside our balcony*. Only horrors! There was a tree rat squatting in the fork of the tree looking very satisfied and chewing on my plump, fat, juicy, fleshy mango. So my dreams and plans disappeared in in an instant.

From Bali—leaving behind such lovely and gentle people and an exotic and beautiful country—we flew on

to Cairns in Australia. Cairns is considered the gateway to Australia's Great Barrier Reef, and our first stop was the Acacia Court form a very comfortable hotel and very close to the town centre. So we did not have far to walk.

Three things spring to mind about our time there. The first was when we were walking across the grass on our way to the sea front. Mike said to me, "Careful where you put your feet, as there are lots of snakes in this area." So I cautiously watched where I trod. What I didn't realise Wise that Mike had dropped slightly behind me and picked up a small stick and tickled the back of my leg. "A snake!" I screamed and took off across the grass faster than a speeding bullet, not stopping until I had reached the road leading to the sea front. Mike was killing himself with laughter and rolling about holding his side. At that time, I didn't think it was funny. But in a few minutes, we were laughing, as I saw the funny side too.

The next incident occurred when we were at the hotel and walked into the lift. Just as the lift doors were closing, a young couple stepped in, and off we sped to our floor. In the lift, the young man said, "Ooooh, I do like your perfume. It's lovely." The girl gave him and me a withering look as he said it again. I said to her, trying to break the icy atmosphere, "I think the flowers you are holding are beautiful." No good—her face was set in stone.

We reached our floor and quickly stepped out. We went to our room, and I was straight away on the phone with our youngest daughter Marie in England. "Hey, Marie," I said. "Guess what? I've met a handsome young man in the lift and he gave me such a compliment. This was very much to his girlfriend's annoyance. The reply came from back the other

end, "You tart!" The response was typical of Marie, always very quick with the replies.

The other memory from our time in Cairns was when we were out on a catamaran heading out to a part of the Great Barrier Reef on a baking and roasting hot Christmas Day. I stayed on the boat, while Mike and others stepped off the back of the vessel to explore the reef. There was a young man all on his own looking rather miserable. We got to talking. It turned out that he had been disowned by his family, as he had not attended his father's funeral. He felt that his father had done nothing for the family, except getting them heavily into debt, and that he had shown no love for his mum or him and his other brothers and sisters. It was now Christmas Day and not a word from any of them.

I replied, "Listen, I am a mum. And I know your mum will call you, no matter what the circumstances." Sure enough, about fifteen minutes after that conversation, his mobile rang, and it was his mum. His expression was one of relief and happiness.

Meanwhile Mike was under the sea taking in the wonders of the coral and brightly coloured fish. The young man stayed with me all afternoon, and on Mike's return, he said to him, "Do you mind if I kiss your wife? She has made me feel so much better?" I explained to Mike about the situation with the young man and his family, and a slightly amused Mike said, "Yes of course you can." So the young man gave me a quick kiss on the cheek and wished us well.

I asked Mike how he'd gotten on snorkelling on the reef. "It was an amazing sight," he said. "I saw fish of every size and colour, and you could swim in and around them. We were warned about swimming too close to giant clams,

for if one closed on your leg or arm, you would be held in a vice-like grip, unable to get away. So we kept them at a healthy distance. The sunlight penetrated deep into the water, so we could see a long way into the depths. It was a truly wonderful experience." He added, "I could see the wonders of God's handiwork close at hand, and it was very special because it was Christmas Day."

The final polish to this memorable trip was that the catamaran's crew were serving Christmas pudding and custard in the baking heat of an Australian midday sun.

The next stop was down to the east coast. Our hotel was the Hotel Mars, looking across the Brisbane River. Originally, we'd planned to meet up with our friends from New Zealand, but they were unable to come. Our main impressions of the city were of the many statues dotted around the streets and parks and the many bridges across the Brisbane River. Our stay there was a short one.

Soon we were on our way to Fiji in the South Pacific Ocean. Our stay was at the Hotel Keswick, which was very upmarket, set in beautiful surroundings and very close to the beach. Flowers of every description were everywhere. Birds of very colourful plumage were in and among the trees and seemed very tame. I suppose they were used to human activity going on all around them.

It was New Year's Eve, and the hotel had organised a party by the pool and cooked meals from all the different countries for the guests who were staying in the hotel. Jamaican was, of course, rice and peas. England was Fish and chips. For the Americans, the Hotel served up hamburgers and Thanksgiving turkeys. Germany was sauerbraten (meaning "sour" or "pickled" roast), a pot roast

made from many different meats, which were marinated in wine, vinegar, spices, herbs, and seasoning. France was beef bourguignon, a stew made of beef braised in red wine and beef broth and seasoned with garlic, pearl onions, some fresh herbs, and mushrooms. Asian I think was chicken stir-fry, beef chow mein, and steamed wild rice. There were many others I can't remember.

This huge feast was served up under the stars and a cool wind blowing in from the ocean. There was a big sign floating on a raft in the bay that read, "Goodbye to the old year." And at the stroke of twelve, the sign changed to "Welcome to the New Year." Everyone who was around the swimming pool was, by then, very merry and started dragging one another into the pool. We were sitting at a table a little farther away, so missed the initial rush of people pushing others in to the water.

Well, having seen that, we beat a rapid retreat into the hotel and watched all the merriment from our hotel window. I must say, I thoroughly enjoyed my national dish again of rice and peas, and Mike enjoyed his fish and chips.

The beach party went on well into the small hours of the morning, and there were very few at breakfast, as the New Year's revelries had caught up with all who had partied the night away. Our stay at the Warwick was soon over.

Our last stop was San Francisco in Northern California, surrounded by the Pacific Ocean and San Francisco Bay and well known for the Golden Gate Bridge, cable cars, and colourful Victorian houses. In the bay sat Alcatraz Island, site of the notorious former prison.

On arriving at our hotel, we were disappointed to see our room overlooked a car park a few stories below and not

a very interesting view. Mike said, "I'll see if I can change this," and took the lift down to reception.

About fifteen minutes later, he was back with a big smile on his face. "Well?" I said. "What happened?"

He explained that he had told the receptionist that the room was fine, but it is our wedding anniversary, and it would be lovely to finish on a high note. "Our last stop in San Francisco at your hotel with a room with great views would be a lovely way to finish an exciting and fabulous world tour."

"Leave it with us, sir," said the receptionist. "I will contact the manager and see if he can come up with something more suitable. In the meantime, don't unpack too much."

An hour later, the phone in our room rang. It was the under manager, saying, "Mr Green, we have found another room for you. But can you please wait until tomorrow to allow the guests who are there to vacate?"

This was fine, and we spent the afternoon looking around the local area and taking in the sights and sounds of the city.

Later the following day, Mike was asked to come to the reception desk and given another card and room number, which seemed to be much higher up the building than our present one. On reaching the new room, we found out that we had been given the executive suite, which took up almost the entire top floor, featuring a lounge, dining room, kitchen, another bedroom, walk-in wardrobes, deep thick pile carpets, and spectacular views across the city. This was a truly amazing way to finish our tour of the countries and islands we had visited.

Our final memory of the trip was crossing the Golden

Gate Bridge on a coach tour. We were told the bridge, when it was first constructed, had not been painted in gold but an orange colour used as a sealant to protect the bridge. It had gotten its name by way of a song, "There's a Silver Moon on the Golden Gate," which was created and sung to commemorate the opening of the bridge in 1933.

We also visited Alcatraz, the famous prison that housed America's notorious criminals. We even went into Al Capone's cell, a tiny room measuring 5 by 9 feet (1.52 metres wide by 2.74 metres in length).

Then later we were on to Fisherman's Wharf, best known for being the location of Pier 39 and the Cannery Shopping Centre. There was the Wax Museum at Fisherman's Wharf and San Francisco Maritime Historical Park. Seafood restaurants were plentiful in the area. We tasted for the first time Dungeness crab and clam chowder served in a sourdough bread bowl. And we saw many other interesting sights.

Eventually, though, our time was up, and after a whirlwind around-the-world tour, we headed for home. Our heads were full of the sights and sounds we had experienced.

On arrival at the check-in desk, I was asked why Mike and I had been to so many different countries in such a short time. Mike explained we were celebrating our wedding anniversary, and as a special treat, we'd decided to take in as many countries as we could. He added that, while in the military, he'd served in some of these countries and wanted to show them to me. The desk clerk smiled, pointed out our seat numbers, and gave us back our passports.

When the call came for our flight back to the United Kingdom, all those boarding dutifully made our way to the

final gate, where we were checked through. On reaching that point, the flight attendant said. "Oh Mr and Mrs Green, your seat numbers have changed and you have been upgraded and will now be travelling first class courtesy of British Airways. Flying back, we were offered champagne and wine. But we settled for soft drinks, as neither of us drinks alcohol, and enjoyed the luxury of being able to settle back in soft roomy individual seats with plenty of legroom. Meals were served with real cutlery, not your plastic variety, and there was a proper glass for whatever you were drinking. It was a superb way to end a very interesting and exciting tour.

We have flown many times since but never with the same degree of comfort. Our method of travelling now is by cruising—a slower but more relaxing style of seeing different places. I wasn't so sure about sailing. But after our first cruise, which was through the Panama Canal with the Royal Caribbean line, I was hooked, and we found a new method of visiting different countries. It is also a chance to dress up, feel good, and look glamorous when we attend formal nights on board. I think this is because of the time when we were at Sandhurst and we had so many social functions to attend. Mike still cuts quite a figure in his tuxedo, and together we feel like king and queen. I realise dressing up is not everyone's dining experience of choice, and there are restaurants on many cruise liners that cater to a more relaxed style of dining.

The farthest we have cruised is down to South Africa to Cape Town and the famous Table Mountain. Travelling to the top is an experience one never forgets, as the mountain flanks and rocks are so close, you think one swing of the

cable car and you will smash into them. When you are at the top, you have this wonderful panoramic scene stretched out 1,085 feet below you. If you are lucky, you will have a cloud-free day like we did. But some days, the top is covered by clouds; when that happens, it's said the mountain has its "tablecloth" on.

While we were on top, I felt very ill, and Mike had to get me off the mountain as quickly as he could. So after a fifteen-day cruise and visiting other countries on the way to South Africa and then the trip to get to the peak, I lasted about fifteen minutes on top and then had to get a cable car back down to the bottom to sit in the coach. I was feeling very sick and sorry for Mike, who had been looking forward to this trip for months.

I could go on to mention other cruises, but I rather think this is beginning to read like a travellers' guide to faraway places. I will mention one more country and then stop. As of this writing, we are off to Jamaica later this year and I can show Michael where I was born, and as a very young child, taken in and adopted by my uncle. It will probably be our last time over there, as we find flying quite demanding and not the relaxed and crowd-free days of yesteryear. There are not many cruises sailing to the Caribbean at the time of the year we want to go, as it will be in the middle of the hurricane season, so we have to fly. We are going to celebrate our fifty-seventh wedding anniversary in Jamaica, the land of my birth, the land where I grew up as a young woman, the land where I met and married my husband.

Now Mike and I are starting to draw together the final part of this story told in two books. *Montego May* (and now *Forward Together*) which started off as a record for my

children, grandchildren, and now great-grandchildren—so they can know how life was lived when we were young. By reading through this book, they can follow our story from our early married lives. Through to middle age, and finally into our more senior years.

Looking back on my life, I count myself very privileged and fortunate that, from a very humble and a poor upbringing, I met and married a wonderful and loving husband. With him, I have had so many interesting and exciting adventures. As a little girl, I used to hear about faraway countries, never ever expecting to see or visit them. I had never seen snow or experienced the cold weather England can produce, bringing the country to a halt. I never thought I would be flying to England in a plane, much less flying one. I never thought I would meet royalty or see some of the queen's family close up at a garden party. If someone had said I would visit Egypt and see the pyramids and even go inside one, climb a Mayan Temple in the Yucatan Peninsula in Mexico, see and climb the Leaning Tower of Pisa in Italy, actually step onto the crust of an active volcano on a Greek island, and visit an opencast gold mine in New Zealand, I would have laughed and thought he or she was mad. There are so many other places we have visited. Some I have mentioned; others I have left out as I said; it was beginning to sound like a tourist guide book.

Our children, Aline, Anthony, and Marie, are a blessing to us, followed by their children, Julia, Neil, Joseph, and Samantha. And now we are into great-grandma and great-granddad time with Haley; Julia; Hazel; and, the latest addition, Elton. Each and every one is very precious to us. We are still active and have health and strength to travel,

to invite friends for dinners or barbecues, and to enjoy our family as we all sit around the dinner table most Sundays.

And finally, a mention of our house. Built in the late '40s by a builder for himself and his sister, it has become a truly wonderful heritage for us. Here, we have raised our children and seen and welcomed our grandchildren and our great grandchildren, all part of the wonderful mix we have of young and old. I remember still the words of an old man who used to live opposite our place, who said a long time ago, "I saw your house being built in the 1940s and early 50s. Since that time, there have always been children running about in your place It is an amazing statement, as it still rings true today, with the sound of laughter and excited chatter echoing throughout the rooms. This house has so many happy memories held within its walls.

I think we have been well and truly blessed. True, we have our ups and downs, as with all families. But looking back over our lives, I know our blessings far outweigh the bad or worrying times. So together Mike and I, as the book title suggests, stepped *Forward Together*. And through the years, we've experienced the highs and lows of life and come through older, stronger, and wiser and still very much in love.

Why are people afraid of getting older? You feel wiser.
You feel more mature. You feel like you know yourself
better. "Yesterday is history, tomorrow is a mystery, today
is a gift of God, which is why we call it the present.

Lilly May

Love is to have someone very special,
one on whom you can always depend
to be there through the years, sharing laughter and tears,
as a partner, a lover, a friend.

Krina Shah

ABOUT THE AUTHOR

Lilly May was born in Jamaica in the late 1930s. She originally wrote her books, first *Montego May* and then *Forward Together*, for her own children as a historical reference. She was brought up by her uncle, who was kind but strict. But by other people, she was taken for granted and lived in near slave-like conditions. Hers is a story of trying to better herself. For years, each job was worse than the one before. She was starved, almost raped, and had to sit at the back of a class because of her uncle's poor income; he could not afford to buy her books for school. There were many more incidents of people being unkind to her, and still she tried her best to please.

She eventually got a job as a housemother working with blind children at the Salvation Army School for the Blind in Kingston. She still had troubles there with the staff, which did the cooking and other tasks around the school.

She eventually met a young soldier from England, and from there, her future became certain. The two are now married and enjoy an extended family of children, grandchildren, and great-grandchildren. She is a very happy person and lives in the United Kingdom.

Printed in the United States
By Bookmasters